TEACHING TO TRANSCEND

TEACHING
TO TRANSCEND

Educating Women against Violence

Cheryl L. Sattler

STATE UNIVERSITY OF NEW YORK PRESS

Published by
State University of New York Press, Albany

For information, address State University of New York Press,
State University Plaza, Albany, NY, 12246

Production by Cathleen Collins
Marketing by Patrick Durocher

Library of Congress Cataloging in Publication Data

Sattler, Cheryl L.
    Teaching to transcend : educating women against violence / Cheryl L. Sattler.
        p.   cm.
    Includes bibliographical references and index.
        ISBN 0–7914–4595–X (alk. paper). — ISBN 0–7914–4596–8 (pb :
        alk. paper)
    1. Wife abuse—United States—Prevention.   2. Family violence—United
States—Prevention.   3. Women—Crimes against—United States—Prevention.
4. Safety education—United States.   I. Title.
HV6626.2.U5 S37 2000
362.82′927′0973—dc21   99–046214
                                                                                CIP

10 9 8 7 6 5 4 3 2 1

In memory of my friend, Dr. Kellie McGarrh,
who was murdered by her partner
November 1995

Never again.

Neither slavery nor involuntary servitude, except as a punishment for crime whereof the party shall have been duly convicted, shall exist within the United States, or any place subject to their jurisdiction.

—Amendment XIII of the U.S. Constitution,
passed January 31, 1865
ratified December 6, 1865

Contents

Preface   xi
A Purposeful Writing   xi

Introduction   xv
Two Shelters, Shared Hope   xx
Organization of the Book   xxi

Chapter 1. Ties that Bind: Domestic Violence as Slavery   1
Go Down, Moses   2
Way Down to Egypt Land   3
Tell Old Pharoh   4
Let My People Go   7
Uneasy Silence   9
From Slavery to Freedom   10

Chapter 2. Education in the Company of Women   13
Women's Work, Women's Space, Women's Refuge   15
From Parlor to Politics   17
Shelters as Communities   20
Through the Shelter Door   23
Settling in to Shelter Life   24

Chapter 3. (Re)gaining Consciousness   27
Telling Stories   32
Raising Consciousness and Raising Hell   35
Consciousness-raising in Shelters   36
A Storm in a Haven   44

Chapter 4. Learning Without Teachers, Teaching Without Books   47
Translating Formal and Informal Learning   52
Defining Spaces as Educational   53
Formal Training   59

There But For the Grace of God   59
Shelter Work as a Teaching Profession   63

Chapter 5. Sharing Secrets and Making Noise   65
The Clothesline Project   67
An Education in Silence   69
Teaching with T-Shirts   73
Thinking Outside the Box   75
Education on the Line   76

Chapter 6. Sisters Doin' It For Themselves   79
Fight for Power   80
Making (Difficult) Choices   82
A Contrast in Control   85
A Place to Call Home   87
(Re)Building Trust   90

Chapter 7. Teaching to Transcend   93
The Meaning of Survival   94
An Unbroken Circle   98

Appendix A. The Dynamics of Domestic Violence   103
Nowhere To Run To   105
Faces of Victims: Faces of Friends   107
Faces of Control: Faces of Men   107
I'm Sorry . . . Forgive Me . . .   109
Out of Control   116
Are You Ready, My Sister?   118
I Wish I Were a Boy   122

Appendix B. Domestic Violence Timeline, with Key Slavery-
Related Dates   125

Appendix C. Teaching and Learning with Adults   129
A Question of Purpose   130
Profile of an Adult Learner and an Adult Educator   132
Redefining the Adult Learner   132
Redefining the Adult Educator   133
From Theory to Practice   134
Feminism and Andragogy   135
Question Assumptions   136

References   139

Index   151

Preface

A Purposeful Writing

I have worked as a feminist activist for years in local communities and national politics. My work has included clinic defense, peacekeeping, local organizing, and working on campaigns. The work that has affected me the most, however, has been my affiliation with domestic violence and rape crisis shelters. As a graduate student, I worked as a hotline counselor; I counseled women in crisis both in the shelter and across a phone line. I remember the particular feeling of my heart racing and of lunging for a pen when the hotline rang. I also remember the sleepless nights when phone calls went dead in my hands, the last sound echoing a woman's scream or, worse, a gunshot.

I never intended to work in the area of domestic violence. I knew nothing about it, even as a feminist activist. It was as a graduate student that, as co-president of the campus National Organization of Women (NOW), I was urged by my co-president to attend an orientation for the training session for the local shelter. It is accurate to say that that night changed my life.

Instead of leaving after that single session, which lasted several hours, I committed to the rest of the 40 hours worth of training. After the training, I worked weekly at the shelter, answering the hotline, counseling women and occasionally children, and became immersed in their lives and in the ways in which societal forces interacted with their personal circumstances to create and reinforce abuse against women, and in so doing vilified the women as well. I worked at the shelter for several years while I completed my doctorate, writing a dissertation on feminist teaching as it is structurally constrained by the spaces in which it is practiced.

During my time there, the women I counseled also counseled me. They encouraged me in my work, often referring to me as "the doctor" as though they collectively identified with my "success." Although I knew about and participated in the kinds of education—feminist education—that took place in the shelter, it was not until a friend asked me what the book I had always wanted to write would be about that I considered joining this highly personal experience with my work on feminist education. My answer was "battered women," and by the time dinner ended, the idea for this book had been articulated for the first time. This is not a book primarily about the struggle for women's safety, or the social ills that perpetuate domestic violence. There are many books written from that perspective, and a brief bibliography of some of those sources is included with this text. This is a book about feminist education.

The kind of education I care about is the kind that changes lives. In the dreadful balance that maintains the lives of battered women, education can make all the difference in saving emotional and spiritual—and all too often physical—lives. This book is about that kind of education, which is profoundly feminist, profoundly engaged with women's lives, and virtually unnoticed by all but the immediate circle of those whose lives have been saved or changed. No school boards fight over this curriculum, and no protesters wave signs or chant rosaries in opposition. There is almost no training in domestic violence to be a "teacher;" instead shelter workers and volunteers from all walks of life teach without teaching, without textbook or classroom. Their "lectures" are punctuated by hotline calls and childrens' cries, by laughter and tears. The theme, however, remains the same: how to save the lives in the balance.

This book is a highly personal exploration for me—as a survivor and an advocate—as well as those women who participated formally in this research. Although I have never been the victim of domestic violence, I have been stalked twice, physically attacked in the presence of onlookers who did not intervene, and I escaped a rape by what I can only call the intervention of the goddess. All the same, my experiences are different from those of the women I have encountered in my work in the domestic violence/shelter movement. However, in my years of working in domestic violence shelters, I have shared in some of the terror these women feel—over the phone, huddled in a shelter office while a strange man drove up, watching my rear-view mirror as I traveled to and from the shelter, worrying about the traceability of my former, highly distinguishable car. I have learned to tell my story, and the story of other women, with jumbled details so that lives are not put into jeopardy. I have learned to ignore women in supermarkets and in drugstores—women I knew as shelter residents—because of my identifiable status as a shelter worker. I have laughed with women in the middle of the night, and I have cried with them, and spent sleepless nights on the phone with the sheriff in the next county arranging safe transport across state lines. It is because I am fundamentally committed to these women and to the cause of both feminist movement and feminist education that I began this project. I write with the intent of bringing the lessons learned from shelters back into other educational environments to intermingle the informal feminist education with the formal and to create a synergy between the two, not-so-separate, worlds.

I did not undertake this journey alone—far from it. I owe sincere thanks to many who walked beside, behind, and in front of me. My husband and soulmate, John Lockwood, is my refuge and my strength. He inherited my past and confronts it daily with charm and grace. Laura Begault, my friend through eternity, answered her phone many late nights. Mike Garet, my friend and colleague, reminds me daily of the joy of intellectual conundrums and inspires me to live on more caffeine and less sleep. Julie Blum and Beck Dunn, directors of women's shelters where I worked, provided access and empathy. The women in this book spoke openly and honestly, weeping and laughing with us, and they make this book both possible and worthwhile. Barbara Ross, then volunteer coordinator at Refuge House, enthusiastically kept me going. Many colleagues at the American Institutes for Research not only cared about this work but celebrated milestones and nudged me toward deadlines; special thanks to Becki Herman for helping in more ways than it's possible to describe. WomenSpirit, and Women With Wings, fabulous groups of souls, provided the final inspiration to finish, and Lee Carpenter brilliantly edited the text when I could no longer distinguish a split infinitive from a split end. Anonymous reviewers and audiences at the American Education Research Association (AERA), particularly members of Research on Women's Education contributed immeasurably, as did the gentle patience and understanding of Priscilla Ross, my editor, and Jennie Doling, her able assistant. You all overwhelm me.

Introduction

I hold my sister with a trembling hand,
I would not let her go!
—Wrestling Jacob, African-American spiritual

The light gray carpet is difficult to keep clean. It is the gift of a church group who could not have predicted that the room would endure the lives of nearly 200 women and their children each year. The children, ranging from day-old infants to sixteen-year-old girls, run through the room in play and in distress, leaving their indelible marks on the worn, spotted rugs. Behind a closed door, a group of women who have left their abusers—some for the first time, some for the last—meet in support groups with counselors and volunteers. This shelter for battered women is one of many sites for women's education. In previous work, I have examined the specific contexts of the university and the high school as sites of feminist teaching. In such formal educational contexts, the educational structures are easily locatable and descriptions of these structures abound in the literature. Informal contexts of education, however, and specifically contexts of feminist education are much less obvious, and therefore much less commonly discussed in conversations about education. Most of what we speak of when we speak of education concerns schooling, that act of attendance and credentialisation by our formal institutions of schools. It is largely compulsory and heavily regulated by various state agencies. Domestic violence education, in contrast, represents a different enterprise, at once an outgrowth of particular feminist political movement. This story, largely untold, focuses on a struggle for women's education and women's freedom from violence, from naiveté, from desperation.

One battle for freedom familiar to almost every American raised in the United States is the struggle for human rights during slavery; the emblem of this movement is the underground railroad. In the era when slavery was a brutal fact of Southern existence, a secret network of individuals formed a passage to the North and to freedom. Houses and other secret locations served as safe spaces for this passage, and the railroad was guided by conductors such as Harriet Tubman; through this secret and dangerous route, many escaped to freedom. In the twenty-first century a similarly structured underground railway exists for women and children who are enslaved by violence. Battered women's shelters[1] with their confidential locations, screening for safety, informal resource networks, and links with other shelters provide the modern equivalent of the slave's railway: a dangerous path to freedom.

At the end of the railway, slaves were assisted with reclaiming lives that had been denied them. They required economic assistance and the support of others. Women in domestic violence shelters have these same needs, and their journey through the railroad is no less dangerous, nor their enslavement any less severe. Every year in America an estimated 3 to 4 million women are beaten by their life partners. Every year, 1,000 women are killed. Women are most likely to be killed when they leave their abusive situations. Yet women do leave, and they do survive, create new lives, and tell their stories. Much of the explanation for the success of this modern railroad lies in feminist education.

In the early days of the feminist movement against domestic violence, "safe homes" provided the majority of space for women to escape. Although they are now run on a somewhat larger scale, domestic violence shelters still tend to be large houses, indistinguishable by design from the surrounding community and families. Historically and in contemporary society, women have created safe spaces for other women for education, whether formally or informally structured. These spaces are often but not always contested, ranging from book and quilting groups to the more overtly political sphere of abortion clinics, women's studies classrooms, rape crisis centers, and domestic violence shelters. Such spaces provide critical education to women, although most of them are constructed outside the realm of formal education. There they have different—sometimes lesser, sometimes greater—constraints than in formal education. The work of Penny Weiss and Marilyn Friedman attests to the power of women's communities (1995). The primary purpose of these spaces is often not overtly to educate participants; however, the spaces created serve multiple purposes, including education, and the practices of workers and participants are pedagogical. Learning takes place.

Shelters, like homes, have many rooms; these rooms are analogous to the processes women go through in shelters. Some women gather around the kitchen stove or sink; others smoke in the living room or congregate in a bedroom or on the stairs. Some confide in counselors in quiet spaces; others

---

1. I use the terms battered women's shelter and domestic violence shelter synonymously throughout.

link with women through mutual reciprocation of child care. These are the rooms of care, nurturance, tears, and realization, full of the mutual education that this book describes. Along with the revelations of counselors, staff, and other residents, posters on the wall often serve as windows to opportunity and other worlds, revealing "women who dared," women's rights, and philosophies and tactics of nonviolence. However, the homes that are, in truth, domestic violence shelters also have basements that darkly house the dirty secrets of domestic violence; it is in these basements that shelter workers dodge the gunshots of batterers, where women and children cry at night, and those fleeing for their lives pass through. If the upper rooms are those in which women gradually piece and stitch the pieces of their lives together, within themselves and with others, the basement is a grim reminder of their need for safety. I am reminded of the all-too-literal colloquialism of a "skeleton in the closet." The women in domestic violence shelters share a common thread: they are in shelter because there is real and present danger in their lives in their own homes or on the street. Here the reason for the modern railroad becomes clear: a war in which women's survival is uncertain, resources are few, and hiding is necessary.

I have focused this book on a particular kind of safe space for the education of women: battered women's shelters. The shelter movement is part of the larger feminist movement in the United States. Since 1975, histories have recorded women traveling from shelter to shelter, seeking safety, space, and answers. Shelter workers, including a large population of volunteers are engaged in counseling, education, the provision of social services, and listening intently to women's stories and helping them regain their lives. Because this feminist work occurs outside of the sphere of formal education, the educational implications of these shelters have not been examined.

Research has highlighted some of the value of other women-oriented spaces such as book groups or quilting circles; however, such research generally examines these spaces in terms of friendship and relationships among women, rather than politicized, radicalizing, educational space. Women's studies research tends to use metaphors such as quilting to illustrate the ties that bind women together; my intent is to delve deeper into the conversation as well as the craft that comprised quilting circles and other women-oriented spaces. The contemporary Clothesline Project borrows from the classical "women's sphere" tradition, combining traditional female icons of "doing the laundry" with bold political praxis—women speaking out from, and against, the pain of violence done to them.

I use these reminders from women's past and present craftwork to illustrate that women have made space for other women since the beginning of known history, and that this same craft tradition characterizes the educational spaces of shelters. Women have traditionally been viewed and located in the domestic sphere, and so the spaces they created for each other were reflective of this sphere. They did "domestic" tasks—but they also in this way created politics. Throughout, social ties were created, the kinds of ties where women understood and cared for women.

Susan Glaspell's short story and play, *Trifles*, is a fictional example of this ethic. In the story, a woman has been accused of killing her husband, despite her reputation as an upstanding member of the community. When a group of men and women gather in the house to deconstruct the rationale for the killing, it is the women who notice the "trifles," the meaning of the unwashed dishes and disarray in the house of a woman known for her well-kept house.[2] It is the women who find the strangled body of the wife's canary in her sewing basket, and who understand that its death was the death of hope and beauty in the house. As women, they decide not to speak up—thereby saving the accused woman's life—and ironically as women, they are simultaneously dismissed as useless by the men (Glaspell 1927). This is the same type of loose social network, where women understand other women and act in their best interests, that equals today's shelters. Shelters represent a "domestic" space that has been (often radically) politicized. Like Glaspell's wives, women in shelter rely on one another's silence.

Shelters are interesting as a particular way in which women not only create literal and psychological safe spaces for other women but the ways in which these political spaces also form educational spaces. In order to understand what this education is like, it is critical to first understand the circumstances under which it takes place. The issues involved in domestic violence are emotionally and physically difficult as well as complex, and there are numerous texts that do justice to these intricacies. In recognition of and deference to the body of literature that has been written by counselors, psychologists, and survivors on domestic violence, a brief appendix provides a concise explanation of the dynamics of domestic violence and battered women's shelters. However, this text is designed primarily for those interested in education, particularly feminist education. Those who are not familiar with domestic violence should consult Appendix A.

Domestic violence shelters operate in a deliberately hidden manner, but they incorporate and expand upon the concepts of feminist pedagogy recognizable in formal education. Among those concepts are intent listening, empowering, voice, and radical social action. Within shelters, women are

---

2. Here I should mention that it is the men who are to "solve" the murder; the women accompany them ostensibly to bring the accused some domestic items that she has requested. A useful analysis of this play by Magda Gere Lewis (1993) reveals that the entire transaction is a communication among the three women: the accused leads the other two to her rationale for the murder, and the other two women agree in the conspiracy.

literally taught concepts from self-worth to financial management, parenting, and feminist values of equality and rights. They also are educated more subtly through counseling, interaction, and affirmation of their own stories and survival. The ways in which these women are educated within the context of an enterprise of rescue informs many current social dilemmas faced in our society; similar dangers and a need for knowledge also are associated with teenage pregnancy, rape, and HIV/AIDS, among others. The application of this work is not only to expand the concept of feminist spaces and feminist pedagogy but to expand our understanding of the connections between education and politics (particularly the political economy of social knowledge) and non-school-based educational spaces.

What does education, even a politicized education, have to do with domestic violence? This question is exactly what I intend this book to address. My goal is to show the potential of education in "alternative" spaces to reach populations who are unreached, or unreachable, by typical educational structures; to convey content that is omitted from traditional curricula; and to push the definition of pedagogy in ways that may be useful to borrow for other educational enterprises. Throughout the centuries, schools have been burdened with ever-increasing responsibilities: to teach religion, health, sex education, driver's education, personal responsibility, conflict resolution, and an endless list. By piling on these responsibilities (and removing few), we reinforce the view of education as society's great panacea. Yet, even in the face of this exploding agenda, schooling has remained largely the same for the past century. The length of the school day and school year as well as learning modalities have remained relatively stable over time. Investigating other environments—here, domestic violence shelters—provides some insight into other ways of dealing with controversial, and dangerous, issues.

Domestic violence is an issue typically addressed within the sphere of counseling or social work. However, domestic violence shelters and other literal "safe" spaces for women comprise part of a much larger, albeit informal, feminist social movement and social structure. They function as part of the feminist movement and feminist education; this work reveals those connections together with a revelation of how shelters function as educational spaces for women. Shelters, like schools, confront demands of multiple agendas: to physically shelter women from abuse; to move them out of shelter to resume their lives; to maintain privacy and security yet meet requirements of government bureaucracy and legal systems. Shelters, like schools, fight for legitimacy. Police often conclude that shelters don't work because women return to their abusers, dismissing domestic violence as "messy," crossing the public/private boundary and disturbing accepted ideas of home and family. Treatment theories vary; should women receive lay counseling, or be considered clients of psychotherapy? Who is targeted for intervention, the abuser or the abused? All of these tensions contribute to the controversy. The careful ways in which women shelter and teach each other in these highly contested spaces, despite and because of the element of real physical danger, transforms the meaning of education at the boundary.

Second, domestic violence crosses all boundaries of race and class as well as socioeconomic status. Although many mistakenly assume domestic violence primarily affects poor women, in reality battered women come from all walks of life, all ages, all races, and all kinds of communities. Many women fleeing from violent situations are well-educated, having traveled through the formal educational system. Some of the women are not. For women in both these situations—"educated" and "uneducated"—shelters must perform a critical educative role about social roles, structures, economic realities, and physical safety. Shelters teach women to understand the system of social services, to find employment, believe in themselves, and define themselves in their own terms. Shelter workers advocate for domestic violence victims in courts, schools, and the community. Battered women who escape their situations sometimes become advocates as well, educating still other women who are finding their way from violence.

The book is derived from participant observation in domestic violence shelters and education as well as first-hand narrative accounts from shelter workers, volunteers, and domestic violence shelter clients. It contributes to the growing literature on feminist pedagogy, an understanding and knowledge base not only of feminist social movement, but the specific contemporary social ill of domestic abuse. Education and domestic violence activism share ideals: a maxim in the shelter movement relates that "domestic violence feeds on silence"; just as surely we in education believe that knowledge is power. Knowledge breaks the silence surrounding women, enabling learning at the boundary of self and other—empowerment education.

I present this education from several perspectives: foremost, the women who have passed through the shelter network and who share the education they received. Second, from the shelter workers who integrate counseling, social service links, and education. Shelter workers teach both battered women and the volunteers who also staff domestic violence shelters. Finally, I present other educational dimensions of shelters, including community outreach and the ties between the education of battered women and feminist education as part of feminist social movement.

Two Shelters, Shared Hope

Of the now hundreds of shelters across the country, I collected data in two: Refuge House, located in Leon County, Florida, and serving a cachment area of seven counties; and My Sister's Place, in Washington, D.C., which serves city residents. Each shelter contains 24 beds, a testament less to the equal needs of these two areas as to the difficulty of securing funding. The data in this book are based on participant observation at both shelters for approximately five years; participation in training at both shelters (both as trainee and trainer); extensive semistructured interviews with 16 domestic violence survivors and seven staff members, about 20 people who viewed the Clothesline Project, six women in Washington, D.C.'s Clothesline Project, and, by e-mail, conversations with college instructors and their students; systematic documentation of service provision over two years at one shelter; and collection and review of documents produced by both shelters.

Interviews resulted in hours of tape, lovingly transcribed by volunteers for My Sister's Place. I then carefully analyzed these transcripts, documents, and other information, searching for themes throughout the women's stories. Each theme developed in this book is firmly rooted in data.

E-mail inquiries to WMST-L, a women's studies list moderated by Dr. Joan Korenman of the University of Maryland, Baltimore County, provided yet more data, particularly on the resonance of the themes I develop in this book with shelters across the country. Throughout the text, I refer to shelters in plural; by doing so, I mean to ground my discussion in the work I have conducted in these two shelters but to extend the argument to other shelters as well.

Clearly, all shelters would not embrace all of the arguments laid out in this text. For example, initial consideration of Rosie's Place, a Boston shelter, offers the contrast of treating women as "guests" rather than making them responsible for chores around the shelter. However, on deeper examination, Rosie's Place also includes a core group much like the two shelters discussed here; in the core group, women not only do chores, but are expected to take action, whether by detox, kicking an addiction, or reentering education or the work force (Cleghorn, 1997). I acknowledge a certain lack of global generalizability; however, I take comfort in the way this work has resonated with domestic violence survivors, shelter workers, and domestic violence researchers who have told me they "see themselves" in this text. I can ask for no more.

Organization of the Book

The book begins with the story of African slavery in the Antibellum South, using the metaphor of the underground railroad to examine not only the dynamics of battering as slavery but to remind readers of the power and daring of escape. Domestic violence shelters are about leaving victimhood behind.

Chapter 2 continues this theme, illustrating that women have, throughout history, acted in their own behalf, despite misconceptions to the contrary. In times when women's place was said to be in the home, women nonetheless created politics out of the ordinary details of their lives. Many times, these politics involved assisting each other, teaching, and learning from one another. Domestic violence shelters draw on these roots in their woman-to-woman structure and belief in the empowerment within the ordinary.

Chapter 3 delves further into the woman-to-woman connection, detailing the consciousness-raising that takes place in shelters, both deliberately and "spontaneously" [although this spontaneity leans heavily on the shelter's structure]. Here, women tell their stories, emerging from their silence not only to speak aloud their own pain but recognizing in the process their connections to other women. Through this process, shelters teach women that violence is not their fault, but rather is greater than the individual.

Chapter 4 reinterprets typical shelter practices through an educational lens as a way of examining how teaching and learning take place outside of traditional settings. Here, I argue that, regardless of whether shelters and shelter workers consider themselves, respectively, educational spaces and teachers, their actions can be interpreted in this way, and that these interpretations are supported by other writings concerning feminist pedagogy.

Chapter 5 examines outcomes; do women leave shelter with greater understanding? Is learning taking place as well as teaching? The chapter describes the ways in which women struggle with practicing their new learning, the inevitable frustration, and the ideal of empowerment in a domestic violence setting. My focus in this chapter is on women's role in creating their own freedom.

Chapter 6 moves beyond shelters, still further into the nonformal education realm. Here, the Clothesline Project illustrates a forum in which women speak out in public, and the ways in which the public react.

Last, chapter 7 asks how women themselves define survival and where their journeys end. Many in shelter have gained the ability to clearly picture a future without violence, without pain. Chapter 7 also returns deliberately to two themes: the politics of the ordinary and domestic violence's connection to slavery. Recent research provides a direct link between women's everyday work, the making of quilts, to slaves' escape and final freedom. This final link underscores the nature of escape: women and slaves help their own, and themselves. They own their escape.

CHAPTER 1

Ties that Bind

Domestic Violence as Slavery

Down on me, down on me
Looks like everybody in the whole round world
Is down on me
—*Down on Me*, African-American spiritual[1]

When I moved to Maryland in 1994, little did I know that I was only a
short distance from where Harriet Tubman, known as "the Moses of
her people," conducted slaves from the Eastern Shore to Canada in search
of freedom. She herself escaped in 1849, and guided slaves to the North
until 1860—more than 100 years before I too walked on the Eastern Shore,
so much like my home in the marshes of Florida. My focus, like hers, was
on slavery, but particularly on women enslaved by domestic violence. I
believe Harriet Tubman would recognize the evils of slavery in the plight of
many supposedly "free" women today.

For most Americans, the word "slavery" automatically conjures the
image of Southern black slavery prior to and during the Civil War. In fact,
slavery has continued to be a reality for many women [and some men]
within this culture, and if the category is broadened to encompass *de facto*
ownership of one person by another, slavery clearly is a modern reality.
Battered women's traditions are strongly tied to those of African-American
slavery; both involve the involuntary slavery of a people[2] and a dangerous

---

1. Although within this text, I argue that slaves could not be considered African Americans
   because of their position within society, the songs used throughout this text are taken from
   the work of Richard Newman. His 1998 text, "Go Down, Moses, A Celebration of the
   African-American Spiritual," names slave songs as belonging to the "African-American"
   race. In deference to his work, when I quote lyrics from his text, I ascribe them to African
   Americans.
2. Jagger argues that women can be considered as a class: ". . . class society as creating broad
   social types of human beings. The nature of individuals is determined not only by the

1

escape, and each has used external assistance together with their own perse-
verance to break their bonds.[3]

My own exploration of these parallels began with the idea of the
Underground Railroad, the secret network of abolitionists willing to assist
runaway slaves. The accounts reminded me of the domestic violence shelter
movement, with its roots in a similar network of feminists rather than abolitionists. As Dawn Bradley Barry summarizes, such networks have long been
part of the subterranean world of women helping women:

> American colonial women organized informal support systems to
> help battered women escape brutal husbands. When the first orga-
> nizers of the American women's movement met in the 1840s for
> the primary purpose of securing the right to vote, the issue of male
> brutality was also on the agenda. Suffragist Susan B. Anthony is
> reported to have helped battered women escape their husbands
> during the same era. (1995, p. 16)

In fact, at the same time that Harriet Tubman and others were conducting
slaves to safety, Martha White McWhirter was founding what may have
been the first shelter, in 1866 (Bradley Berry 1995). However, the clandes-
tine nature of the escapes by both women and slaves—by far the most obvious comparison—provides only one parallel. Also central to this discussion
are the means and definitions of escape, and the similarity of shelters to stations on the Underground Railroad. Slavery and domestic violence share
three key characteristics: bondage; enforced silence; and denial of resources,
discussed here in terms of education or information. Escape requires breaking free from each of these limitations, thus defining the task of both movements against violence against women and against slavery.

Go Down, Moses

The Underground Railroad, named in a time when slaves were beginning to
disappear "as though they'd gone underground," and when the railroad
was a new invention, relied on the abolitionist tendencies of the Quaker
Society of Friends as the backbone of its activism. Consisting of "stations,"

---

of production that prevails in the society they inhabit but also by their place within the
class system of that society" (1988, p. 56). I extend this to incorporate women into "a people," as slaves were so often referenced.

3. The categories of "women" and "slaves" overlap, of course, as women as well as men
    were enslaved in this country. However, in this analysis, I separate the categories for ana-
    lytic purposes; the "women" in this writing are technically "free," although as the analysis
    reveals, this freedom is rhetorical rather than real.

or houses where fugitives would be sheltered, it stretched from Texas to Maine and from Florida to Minnesota. Most slaves fled north, to free states, although others fled south, over the Mexican border or to the Florida swamps. When northern states no longer provided safe haven, slaves traveled even further, crossing the border into Canada. Many times slaves had to depend on their own ingenuity to travel from station to station and received minimal assistance in the form of transportation, food, and guidance. The role of conductors such as Harriet Tubman was to ensure that passengers on the railroad—who traveled at night, through the woods, largely on foot—made it from station to station, and finally to the north, often Canada (Ann Petry 1955; Buckmaster 1992).

The shelter movement, although also rooted in Colonial America, began in earnest in the 1970s in concert with the expansion of U.S. women's movement. Although it originated as a network of safe houses, much like the stations on the Underground Railroad, the movement solidified into formal shelters, which, borrowing techniques from rape crisis centers, formed hotlines, support groups, legal aid centers, and advocacy projects. However, although the movement professionalized, it retains key characteristics of the Railroad. Although they are now run on a somewhat larger scale, domestic violence shelters still tend to be large houses, indistinguishable by design from the surrounding community and families (Bart and Moran 1993; Jones 1994; Schechter 1982). These houses depended on secrecy in much the same way as the stations on the Underground Railroad.

Shelters also provide a web of safe places across the country. Anna Quindlen recently fictionalized this aspect in her book, *Black and Blue,* in which she reveals the existence of extended networks into which a battered woman can disappear and emerge in a new location with a new name and, it is hoped, a new chance. I myself have arranged for such transfers, coordinating transport across state and county lines, in the middle of the night.

Like the FBI's witness protection program, such work has significant drawbacks. As an extreme measure, such tactics are generally invoked when a woman has little other chance to escape pursuit and death at the hands of her abuser. To "go underground," a woman must give up her family, friends, personal property, and all things that serve to identify her. This loss of community and identity is painful (Bart and Moran 1993). Escaping slaves may have undergone this loss, too, giving up their homes and sometimes families for unfamiliar surroundings in return for a chance, but not a guarantee, of freedom.

Way Down to Egypt Land

Harriet Tubman would sing, "Go Down, Moses," to announce her arrival to slaves ready to escape; women's shelters then, as they do now, may have used similar code words to assist women without endangering the women's lives. *The Drinking Gourd* provides a noteworthy example. A familiar story in slavery, the song's lyrics provide secret directions to freedom:

> *The riverbank makes a very good road*
> *The dead trees will show you the way...*
> *Follow the drinking gourd.*
> *The river ends between two hills*
> *Follow the drinking gourd.*

In the song, the drinking gourd refers to the Big Dipper, whose North Star remains a constant reference point in the sky. Some identify the river, which ends between two hills, as the Tombigbee River in Mississippi; other lyrics covertly name the path along the Tennessee and Ohio Rivers, which marked the boundary between the "slave states" and the "free states"—the land of Caanan, the promised land (Buckmaster 1992; Ann Petry 1995; Richard Newman 1998). Codes provide some measure of safety in an unsafe enterprise. Shelters often name themselves in code: Hubbard House (Old Mother Hubbard); House of Ruth ("Whither thou goest, I shall go . . ."); My Sister's Place (a euphanism complex enough to confuse most!).

Secrecy is as important now as it was then. In some shelters, women are not given the address; instead, they are given directions, sometimes partial ones, after which they must call back and receive further instructions. They are instructed not to write down the name of the shelter together with the telephone number. This convoluted process is intended to ensure that women are not followed and that should directions be left behind in a hurried escape, other women will not be endangered (Refuge House 1992).

Tell Old Pharoh

The shelter network and the Underground Railroad share a number of features based in their construction outside the normative discourse of ownership, power, and control, central dynamics both within slavery and domestic violence. The Underground Railroad literally defied the laws requiring the return of slaves to their owners. In 1787, at the Constitutional Convention in Philadelphia, the "fugitive slave and felon clause," giving slave owners a legal basis for retrieving fugitives, was introduced and later became Article IV, clause 2, of the U.S. Constitution. The United States went so far as to ask Canada, a refuge for many escaped slaves, for assistance in returning slaves; Canada refused (Buckmaster 1992; Ann Petry 1955).

Domestic violence has a somewhat more complex and convoluted legal history. While few laws *condone* family violence, there is a widespread tolerance and acceptance, particularly in the legal system, of noninterference in "domestic affairs" (Bart and Moran 1993; Buzawa and Buzawa 1996; Jones 1994; Crowell and Burgess 1996; Schechter 1982). The narratives by survivors of domestic violence echo this again and again (Bart and Moran 1993; Buzawa and Buzawa 1996; Jones 1994; National Research Council 1996; Schechter 1982). Jane Wells's true story, *Run Jane Run* (1996), recounts in more than 300 pages her brutalization, first by her husband and then by the legal system. In ride-alongs with police on their beats, I learned that there is little police dread more than "a domestic," which many view as a private matter rather than a crime.

The abuse also finds inadvertent reinforcement in friends, neighbors, colleagues, relatives, medical staff, and others, who "keep women in line." As Magda Gere Lewis describes it,

> The power of patriarchy is such that the "refusal of the designated other to be dominated is felt as a personal assault" (Williams 1991, p. 66) by those who, from their position of power, initiate the violence. It seems that not the violation but our acts of self-defense come to be read as "antisocial" behavior and are thus used to reposition us on the disadvantaged side of the gender binary. In this case the power of the oppressor is such that it can create social support for acts of violence, a support that in turn justifies the use of more violence to counter challenges to the oppressor's power to violate." (1993, p. 33)

This dynamic reinforces the false notion that women deserve violence, either explicitly through dismissal, doubt, or denial; or implicitly, by the failure to provide assistance (Bart and Moran 1993; Jones 1994; Schechter 1982) (see Appendix A). This network has yet a more invidious aspect, composed of friends of the abuser—often a family who doubts the reality of abuse, or friends in the police force who ensure that charges are not filed, or someone who knows the location of the shelter where she hides. The question typically asked of battered women is, Why didn't you seek help? The answer is obvious.

> "Why didn't you seek help?" I did. Early in our marriage I went to a clergyman who . . . told me that my husband had meant no real harm, that he was just confused and felt insecure. . . . Next time I turned to a doctor. I was given little pills to relax me and told to take things a little easier. I was just too nervous. . . . I turned to a friend, and when her husband found out, he accused me of either making things up or exaggerating the situation. She was told to stay away from me. . . . I turned to a professional family guidance agency. I was told there that my husband needed help and that I

should find a way to control the incidents. . . . At the agency I
found I had to defend myself against the suspicion that I wanted to
be hit, that I invited the beatings. . . . I did go to two more doctors.
One asked me what I had done to provoke my husband. The other
asked if we had made up yet. I called the police one time. They not
only did not respond to the call, they called several hours later to
ask if things had "settled down." I could have been dead by then!
(Del Martin 1976/1995, pp. 46–47)

The need for objective intervention persists. Domestic violence's complexity
marks it as a uniquely intricate, and difficult, crime. The dynamics of
domesticity and violence seem contradictory; domesticity connotes peace,
not conflict, yet contains both. Women flee violence, yet remain connected
to their partners and their need for peace and harmony. Typically, such
internal conflict results in women's multiple returns to abusive partners.
This series of actions tends to be met with a jaded reply from police: "it's
just a domestic," implying that intervention is worthless. If a woman
returns to violence, who is responsible for the outcome? Few victims of
other crimes return to the perpetrator, while this forms a common dynamic
in domestic violence; when victims do return, crimes tend to be personal
and emotionally difficult, such as battering and rape. Understandably,
police and other law enforcement officers become frustrated with the ambi-
guity of such cases. Nonetheless, complex crimes demand no less justice.

As an issue, domestic violence has not often found or placed itself on
center stage in general knowledge, or in studies of education; although the
issue exists and is addressed within the feminist political movement, it is not
recognized in proportion to its effects on women. Because of all of these
silences, many misunderstand or ignore domestic violence as a minor or
peripheral issue, despite overwhelming evidence to the contrary.

Every 12 to15 seconds, a woman is beaten by her partner in the United
States (Dawn Bradley Berry 1995). In fact, battering is the single major
cause of injury to women; this exceeds rapes, muggings, and automobile
accidents combined (William French Smith 1983). In the United States, a
woman is more likely to be assaulted, injured, raped, or killed by a male
partner than by any other type of assailant; one of every two women is battered at some time in her life (NCADV). If a lecture hall full of students
stood up one by one, every 15 seconds in recognition of this crime, it would
take only 25 minutes for 100 to stand; less than an hour for 200; and in 4
hours, 1,000 students would be standing. This 1,000 would represent only
one-sixth of the women who are beaten each day in the United States, and
the approximate number of women who die at the hands of their abusers
each year. These women are our students, our daughters, our sisters, our

colleagues, our neighbors, and our friends. If these statistics are shocking, consider the women behind them, who exist in unrecognized numbers and familiar faces.

Let My People Go

It is no coincidence that slaves and battered women chose similar routes of escape; the dynamics of both settings are remarkably similar. The fundamental dynamic of both slavery and domestic violence is ownership of one human being by another.[4] In slavery, such a relationship was clear: slaves were literally bought and sold at auction; could be bartered to pay off debts; and had no property or personal rights of their own. Slaves could not even claim the rights to their children. What is shocking is that, as Dawn Bradley Barry relates, laws relegating slaves to be the property of their masters were based on common understandings about women:

> In British, American, and many other societies . . . a woman was not a full human being, but property, first of her father, then of her husband. In fact, this idea was so widely accepted by the seventeenth century that the early American slaveholders adopted the law governing women to establish the legal status of slaves! (1995, pp. 17–18)

Ownership is synonymous with power and control.

Other parallels extend this analogy. Slave-holders (masters), barring some notable exceptions, exercised their power cruelly; male domestic partners (husbands, fiancees, boyfriends) exert violence against their female partners (wives, fiances, girlfriends). Many slave narratives render detailed accounts of the abuse and suffering slaves underwent at the hands of their masters. Slaves had no choice about their entry into slavery. Kidnapped from their homeland, they were sold into slavery. Children born to slaves were subsequently born into bondage. Masters had total power over the lives and treatment of slaves, exercising that power by separating families, physically and sexually abusing slaves, and treating African and Carribbean[5] people as subhuman, failing to attend to the most fundamental physi-

---

4. Slaves were not considered to be fully human, as Article I of the U.S. Constitution makes clear. This article provides the formula for calculating congressional representation; slaves counted as three-fifths of a person. However, rather than perpetuate a racist stereotype, I refer to slaves as humans, which they clearly were.

5. These two locations were the primary source for the slave trade. At that time, these involuntary immigrants (Ogbu, 1978) were not African Americans, or Caribbean Americans, for a number of reasons. They had no rights within American society and had not intermingled to any great extent with "native" Americans.

cal needs for clothing, shelter, food, and health care (Buckmaster 1992; Ann Petry 1955). Slaves underwent nearly constant abuse. They had no hope except that their master, when he died, would grant their freedom in his will (manumission).

Similarly, a number of first-hand accounts of domestic violence survivors detail with painful accuracy the daily hurts and indignity of their lives (Martin 1989; Turner 1993; Wells 1996). In domestic violence settings, men exercise total power over the lives and treatment of women and children through economic, physical, and psychological control (Bart and Moran 1993; Buzawa and Buzawa 1996; National Research Council 1996; Jones 1994; Schechter 1982). Those familiar with the dynamics of domestic violence will recognize the power of denying education and communication to women. Slave owners, upon discovering that drums were used by slaves to communicate across plantations, banned their use. Later, they banned singing particular songs linked to escape (*Go down, Moses* was one) and talking among slaves, and any slave who learned to read or write had his or her right index finger severed (Buckmaster 1992; Ann Petry 1955). In *Run Jane Run*, (1996) Jane Wells writes of her abuser ripping the telephone from the wall, questioning all her friendships, and dialing the last number she had called to check up on her. This scenario plays out in different shapes and forms across violent relationships.

However, women do exercise a choice in entering a relationship; this fact often serves as an accusation as well: "She could have left." However, women enter relationships with abusive men under false pretenses, without enough information. Society constructs and reinforces unbalanced relationships in women's favor prior to the formal relationship, that work against them later. For example, what can be mistaken for chivalry or jealousy while a couple is dating can later be revealed as control. Men become violent after relationships are established, when it is difficult to walk away.[6]

Another key difference between battered women and slaves is the false hopes extended to women. The cycle of violence ensures the juxtaposition of their relationship at its worst and then at its best, simultaneously directing her to go, and to stay. This difference between the slaves' situation and that of battered women is critical; slaves could never go back; they knew with certainty that to do so would mean death. Women return to their abusers, sometimes many times, believing in hope—and often denying the signs that to return means death.

---

6. The idea that women should "just walk away" contributes in no small measure to prejudice against battered women. The dynamics of domestic violence, however, complicate this act; see Appendix A.

This comparison between slavery and domestic violence is not yet complete. Slaves, at the end of the Railroad, crowded into schools designed by free blacks to teach them to read and write. In order to translate escape into freedom, they needed education. The end of the Railroad was not the end of their struggle for freedom. Escape, although the most dramatic part of their experience, was not sufficient. Having overcome not only the physical bondage and enforced silence, they also had to find information, education for survival. This is the case for battered women as well. The book's title is taken from the idea that education allows women to transcend their abuse and to translate escape into freedom.

Few know the role education plays in women's escape. The Railroad analogy provides insight into the condition of women's lives when they arrive in shelters, similar to understanding a student's home life as it affects her schooling. Further, it reinforces the dimensions of volition, the courage necessary to escape. This point is critical: most literature concerns women running away. Slave stories lend perspective on *the courage it takes to run*. When women arrive in shelter, then, they are on the one hand battered; on the other hand, they are brave and resourceful. Both of these conditions set the terms for what becomes feminist education in shelters.

As the roots of these two movements are similar, so are the misperceptions about them. For example, the metaphor of "Moses" rescuing "his" people extends to domestic violence as well. First, it harkens back to the fundamental ownership problems embedded within both slavery and domestic violence. Are slaves, and women, "rescued," only because they "belong" to someone else? Second, and more important, it incorrectly focuses on action *on behalf of* women and slaves, *by others*. In reality, both shelters and the Underground Railroad were begun and maintained by victims themselves, albeit with the assistance of others (Buckmaster 1992; Tobin and Dobard 1999). This represents a great irony, as the act of leaving—when both women and slaves were and are in the most danger—portrays both groups as passive victims who would never have succeeded without help. Denial of the courage and fortitude that leaving entails is tantamount to reinforcing the learned helplessness that is a key component of slavery and domestic violence. In this work, I hope to disentangle these misunderstandings.

Uneasy Silence

The reality of both slavery and domestic violence in America, like our history of race, class, and gender privilege, has long been muffled in a painful, uneasy silence. People have suffered in silence and where possible have escaped—again, in necessary silence. Current laws in the United States declare that African Americans, as former slaves, are free; yet there exists a reluctance to discuss slavery, to make reparations, to acknowledge our role and complicity. And, even as the African-American slaves were [nominally] released, other populations—in this work, women of all classes, races, colors, and creeds—continued, and continue, to be enslaved in silence. The perpetuation of domestic violence fundamentally depends on this silence, and in part this silence also binds battered women's experience to that of the slaves.

In the case of domestic violence, the silence stems from a society that turns an unseeing eye through the legal system, judicial systems, and social services. Social structures reinforce the right of individual action and, particularly, the right to privacy. As a society, the strength of our belief in privacy virtually precludes another resource from battered women—the intervention of a stranger (Bart and Moran 1993; Jones 1994). Silence is also inherent in the way our judicial system differentiates domestic crimes from other crimes as though domestic crimes were not real crimes at all, but individual issues. The silence stems from ignorance or denial by otherwise concerned citizens. And the silence arises fundamentally from the women themselves who are trapped within violent relationships without many of the resources necessary to escape.

From Slavery to Freedom

The purpose of this book is to reveal the educational and transformative potential of the "end of the railway" for battered women: the teaching, and learning, for and by women, that takes place in domestic violence shelters, and that can make the difference between suffering and survival. This is a book about the feminist education created within shelters, offered to and given by women who are victims and survivors of domestic abuse.

Throughout the work I maintain the link between domestic violence and slavery, both to invoke the power of this analogy and to provide insight into the dynamics of domestic violence. Slavery reminds us of the difficult journey necessary for escape, as well as the fortitude of those escaping. May we look back at domestic violence tomorrow as we look back on slavery today: with horror and regret.

Slavery also provides a reference to communities, a second theme throughout this work. The Underground Railroad depended on slaves helping slaves, from singing songs of hope and deliverance to teaching reading and writing. The domestic violence network is grounded in this same kind of community, where women teach each other the subtle dimensions of escape through ordinary activities. Later in the book, these two groups, slaves and battered women, become inseparable, sharing the key to the cipher of freedom.

The implications of women's learning in shelter extend outward both in terms of activism and education, as illustrated through the Clothesline Project. In short, this work invokes the struggles of two groups, one in the past and one in the present, offering one way of viewing education as the practice of freedom.

CHAPTER 2

Education in the Company of Women

> If anybody asks you what's the matter with me,
> Just tell him I say
> I'm running for my life.
> —*I'm Running For My Life*, African-
> American spiritual, ca. 1848

Maslow, who organized human needs by priority, tells us our funda-mental need is shelter. It is easily demonstrated that higher goals lan-guish in the absence of shelter and other basic needs. Not surprisingly, women enter temporary shelter not as an act in itself, but as a stepping stone to seek permanent shelter. This fundamental need, more so than desire or any other force, pushes women into domestic violence shelters. But the definition of shelter also inherently implies safety; shelter from the enemy as well as the elements.

The safety inherent in shelter assumes paramount importance to those subject to slavery; here, still more parallels between domestic violence and the Underground Railroad arise. First, shelters and stations on the Underground Railroad are contested ground. They are spaces of danger as well as escape. They place both fugitives and those who shelter them in jeopardy. While women arrive laden with the violence(s) that drive them to seek shelter, slaves brought the threat of slave-catchers and legal repercus-sions. Like slaves eluding capture, women enter needing safety, but are accompanied by danger. Women enter shelter needing solace, but enjoy lit-tle calm. Slaves' journeys were also fraught with danger, hastily conducted in the darkness. Both groups' actions require quickness and agility in the most anxious of situations. Women face the pressure of time, as shelters are short-term solutions at best; a *long* stay might be four to seven months. Stations on the Railroad provided only short-term shelter; only by reaching the North could slaves relax slightly. Slave-catchers patrolled borders for runaway slaves, returning them to slave masters in return for bounty for the catcher, punishment for the slave. Once a slave reached the North, freedom could be stripped from even rightfully freed slaves, as slave-catchers invaded the North, capturing African Americans for resale. By escaping an abusive marriage, women may lose their children, jobs, and rights to their personal property. Survival forces truly high-stakes learning and decision making.

Despite the dangers, shelters and stations provide the only measure of safety available. Partly because of their contested nature, women enter shelters cautiously, and are accepted cautiously, because one woman's survival depends on the safety and silence of the next. Safe space is invoked from the moment of the first call to a shelter hotline: women are told that the shelter is confidential, secret, safe. No one can find her there. It is the space behind the cabinet, under the cellar door, in the corner of the barn, spaces where Railroad participants hid silent women away until dark. It is also one of the few paths to survival.

To ensure this degree of safety, women are given rules to follow when coming to shelter: no one must know the location; she must not contact her abuser; she must not place other lives in jeopardy. Shelter directions are given in partial forms, not unlike a detective or mystery novel in which clues lead to other clues, and only in a roundabout way to a solution. Volunteers are cautioned that this silence must extend around them no matter where they go: the simple act of acknowledging a shelter resident, former or present, in a shopping mall might be enough to make either of them a target, if the volunteer is recognized as a link to the shelter.

These acts reach beyond simple assurances of safety. They are ritual reassurances in which shelter workers, volunteers, and residents wrap themselves, to vouchsafe their own lives. Similar characteristics are woven throughout *The Story of Jane*, Laura Kaplan's retelling of "the legendary underground feminist abortion service." Kaplan relates the ritual of naming all the women in the group "Jane," for a variety of reasons including safety:

> Jane seemed a good choice. No one in the group was named Jane and Jane was an everywoman's name—plain Jane, Jane Doe, Dick and Jane. The code name Jane would protect their identities while protecting the privacy of the women contacting them. Whenever they called a woman back or left a message for her, they could say it was Jane calling. No one else would know what the call was about. (1995, p. 27)

Despite the fact that shelters have, through the years, suffered somewhat less than abortion clinics, which by their very nature are public spaces, both rely on secrecy. I watched the domestic violence community in Florida collectively shudder after learning that shots were fired at Hubbard House, the shelter in Jacksonville. An abuser, learning of the location, appeared at the door and demanded his wife. When she did not appear, the man shot out the locks in the front door and entered the shelter, to the jeopardy of all residents and workers inside. Worse, he violated the confidentiality of the shelter location for the future.

In an almost ironic twist, safety demands other rules: no weapons, no drugs, no unaccompanied minors in shelter. Each of these would endanger all of the women present. It is the weapons clause at one shelter that stays in my mind. One night, past midnight, I answered a call from a woman who had left her husband that night. He had loaded his truck with guns and told her that when he returned from work that night, he was going to kill her. In desperation, she followed him to work, smashed the window of his truck, stole his guns, and called the shelter. As I took her frantic call, reciting the rules and structure of shelter (it's a big house, we share chores, no drugs, no guns) she related what she had done. I will never forget shivering in the dark yard with a sheriff's deputy, waiting for the truckload of rifles the deputy would dismantle. It is necessary, to work at a shelter, to forget or pretend to forget that shelters exist because women are hunted. And that standing in the way of a hunter and his prey can get you shot.

Women's Work, Women's Space, Women's Refuge

In addition to the psychological elements of danger, fear, and the necessity of speed, shelters have a number of key features that predominate this discussion as well as the narratives of the women.

- Shelters are small—often fewer than 20 women and children.
- Shelters are cross-generational, with women of all ages and life experiences.
- Shelters are intimate settings by virtue of their size and house-like settings.
- Shelters group women across race, ethnicity, and language.
- Women stay in shelters for a short period of time, ranging from a day to a few months, but in general their time is about two months.
- Finally, shelters have varying amounts of structure in terms of standard "curriculum," house rules, and guidelines.

Shelters rise from a tradition of "private," "domestic" spaces, those single-sex spaces and connections formed across backyard clotheslines and borrowed sugar. Women have, throughout history, created politics within and outside of the "domestic" space that was their allotted purview. Women used politics, influencing or taking action through personal and group action against wrong or intolerable situations. Many women took action informally rather than challenging the social order, according their actions a higher chance of success. Women assisted each other with abortifacents, intervened in domestic disputes, and exchanged knowledge about birth control, acceptable sexual practice, medicinal remedies, and child care. Sometimes these politics resembled intricately pieced Amish quilts, rigidly ordered, as when matrons proscribed social regulations; more often they were the patchwork of my grandmother, who pieced together any resource she could find.

"Necessity," it is said, "is the mother of invention." My grandmother, too poor to replace a faded tail light, painted its interior with cherry-red nail polish and passed inspection. Through fiction and history, there is a long line of women, like my grandmother, who have worked to liberate women, inventing solutions and spaces where there had been none. Women like my grandmother, operating singly and together, have invented many things—perhaps the most powerful of which is space for one another apart from the frenzy of social expectations and traditional roles. This creation of educational space is part of the domestic violence movement, as well as the history of the larger feminist movement. Like the women they were intended to serve, these spaces adapted multiple forms and functions, from the most ordinary to extraordinary. Such spaces layered multiple functions, often serving an important educational role because they were comprised of women with one purpose but who remained open to many others. Careful examination of these spaces challenges traditional ideas of educational settings.

Consider the elements of teaching and learning within the traditional teaching of women's craft from woman to woman as one example of how education can be framed differently than the traditional schools-teachers-students model. I have recently become interested in quilts, not only for their patterns and intricacy but for the women they represent. *The Quilters*, a play about women during the Western expansion, lovingly illustrates the development of different patterns from the minutiae of women's lives: flying geese, fence rail, log cabin. Pierce and Suit tie past with present, noting: "Early quilts were pieced together from the remnants of daily life and warmed our sleep; art quilts pull together the threads of modern life and warm our souls" (1994, foreword). Here, the ordinary becomes extraordinary.

I never learned to sew as a young woman, disparaging any domestic, "feminine" skill. Today, though, I turn to other women for instruction in quilting and search for the community I hope will follow. Sewing settles me in my family's traditions. Years ago, my grandmother crafted "crazy quilts" out of scraps of my childhood clothing—the dress with the pink parasols I was so proud to wear in my preschool picture; my mother's 1970s Easter dress with its psychedelic swirls; the pieces of my life. If she were here, she would be piecing my wedding quilt with me, saving the remnants of my dress for another creation. My mother recently created a quilt for me as well; I tell my house guests about it as I put them to bed. I tell them the stories of women's spaces, of my mother and my grandmother—of my icons and emblems of the space that women have created.

My grandmother's and mother's quilts are echoed in the work of Faith Ringgold, who moves the idea and ideology of quilts from the simple metaphor of women, stitching together—women who have been called [albeit in jest] the Women's Sewing Circle and Terrorist Society—to quilts that tell more literal stories. Ringgold's story quilts draw the viewer into her space, the space of women's and children's stories, and their lives. Her quilts teach more than appliqué techniques; they tell the story of family, community, of longing and sadness, of happiness and being together, without fear or prejudice. Her quilts tell the story of the women in this work—of piecing their lives together out of leftover scraps and memories, and of using quilts to echo "an important motif in African-America folk-tale literature, in which slaves told of 'flying' to freedom as wish fulfillment or as a metaphor for escaping from slavery" (Broude and Garrard 1994; Ringgold 1995; Tobin and Dobard 1999). The stories of the women living in this book, facing violence in their lives, form part of this long tradition of women's craft and women's space, stitching their lives together, looking for freedom.

From Parlor to Politics

Although this work is not a historical treatise, it is useful to think back through our mothers, as Virginia Woolf suggested, to trace the relationships that brought about domestic violence shelters (formerly, battered women's shelters) in today's U.S. society. The theory of separate spheres introduced by Rosaldo although now widely disputed, gave birth to the concept of "domestic space" as that space occupied by women, largely in the home. However, in an exhibition in the Smithsonian Institution's Museum of American History, the signage argues that home spaces were more permeable than generally ascribed: "the parlor was the space within the home where private life and public life met." The very notion of "parlors" implied a particular class of women, largely those in the middle to upper class. In addition, the events to which they refer took place in the late 1890s, with the beginnings of women's suffrage and their more formal, or deliberate, involvement in politics. Nonetheless, prior to that time, women of all races and classes were still involved in politics. As a domestic referent to the realm of national politics, quilters named their new patterns after presidential politics, choosing sides and platforms (Duke and Harding 1987).

Women's other "domestic" work was similarly revealing. Andrea Atkin (1997) writes of a "porous border" between the public and private

realms. Their work points out the influence of women both in the private
sphere (as in personal influence on friends and spouses) and the public
sphere. Even women's early friendships were political, according to
Freedman:

> Private "sisterhoods," Nancy Cott has suggested, may have been a
> precondition for the emergence of feminist consciousness. In the
> late nineteenth and early twentieth centuries, intimate friendships
> provided support systems for politically active women, as demon-
> strated by the work of both Blanche Cook and Nancy Sahli.
> (1995, pp. 86–87)

One way in which these women crossed the border between the two
spheres, according to Atkin, was through domestic objects like pincushions
and needlebooks, on which they imprinted messages and images meant to
influence (e.g., pillows might proclaim the virtues of a political candidate).
In some ways this activity perfectly encapsulates the role of women in early
politics: they created small, pragmatic objects, leveraging their status as
moral influences (untainted by the world outside their homes), to plow personal inroads into politics. Atkin points out that these acts were at once
both radical and conservative. This above all describes the essence of the
early women's movement.

Early women's groups were naturally the most reflective of the "domestic" sphere [or have been perceived through scholarship this way]: largely
charitable, social, or literary groups, their politics was of a personal nature
(recapitulated, interestingly, in the consciousness-raising groups of the
1970s; see chapter 3). From these early groups, clubs were formed, followed
by programs for community improvement and reform. Freedman writes that
the progression illustrates the politicization of women's institutions:

> The exclusion of women reporters from the New York Press Club
> in 1868 inspired the founding of the first women's club, Sorosis.
> The movement then blossomed to dozens and later hundreds of
> localities, until a General Federation of Women's Clubs formed in
> 1890. . . . Although club social and literary activities at first
> appealed to traditional women who simply wanted to gather with
> friends and neighbors, by the turn of the century women's clubs
> had launched civic reform programs. Their activities served to
> politicize traditional women by forcing them to define themselves
> as citizens, not simply as wives and mothers. (1995, pp. 90–91)

Women expanded outward into the religious domain, leveraging their
domestic roles for a voice in politics. Women's formal entrance into politics—through their parlors—involved issues that were seen as symbolic of

family values in public life. These women argued that the home was affected by the society that surrounded it; as the Smithsonian notes: "Women reformers used their concern for home and family as a justification to take place in politics." This concern led to women's founding of, and participation in, a variety of formal political organizations beyond their "suffrage parlors." These organizations included women's clubs, the temperance crusade, women's suffrage societies, women's trade unions and consumer leagues, all of which served as alternative political parties or sites for social change. These groups were not insubstantial; by 1910, membership was over 1 million (Freedman 1995); and by 1915, collective memberships were as large as 3 million (*Smithsonian* 1996). These groups utilized networking as their powerful basis for social change. Some of their changes included child labor laws, Americanization of immigrants, abolition, labor unions, and health care, as well as kindergartens and education. They claimed that "politics is housekeeping on a grand scale" (*Smithsonian* 1996). Later, women's politics was institutionalized, notably by the nineteenth Amendment granting women suffrage but also by organizations such as Hull House, founded in 1889 by Jane Addams and Ellen Gates Starr. Hull House was, quite literally, the use of "domestic space"—a former home—as a setting for reform (in this case, in the settlement movement). The use of a home itself as a settlement represented a female-defined domestic space enabling women to use—and reclaim—gender concepts as a source of empowerment. As the *Smithsonian* concludes:

> Between 1890 and 1925, women developed a powerful political language and imagery, applying the values of home and family to public life. While women's political culture empowered them at this period and served as a bridge from the private to the public sphere, it also set patterns and boundaries for women's political participation that have continued to the present. (*Smithsonian* 1996)

More recent times present a similar dynamic: "[o]n August 26, 1970, the fiftieth anniversary of passage of the Nineteenth Amendment granting women the suffrage, women from all over the country joined in support of the Women's Strike for Equality" (Klein 1984, p. 1). She tells us that:

> housewives, secretaries, lawyers, mothers, grandmothers, and students were drawn together out of a sense of injustice, personal frustration, and the need to change inequities in the treatment of women. (1984, p. 1)

(For a timeline of the women's movement from 1970 to 1992, see *Ms.* magazine, July 1992; see also *The Women's Political Action Group*, 1992.)

With such a history of women's movement around "domestic" issues, it is no surprise that women also spearheaded the movement against violence within the home, so-called domestic violence. These original networks of women, concerned with social issues, link the present with the past: the anti-slavery movement, embodied in the Underground Railroad; and the eventual social network of women who formed the shelter movement for battered women as well as the underground web of information on abortion clinics. In some ways, only the language has changed: instead of women's clubs, the 1970s had consciousness-raising and affinity groups; the 1990s has women's organizations. The networks of concerned women are the same, embodied in different individuals and, with time, somewhat expanded causes.

Shelters as Communities

Like their earlier female and feminist counterparts, shelters rely on the tasks associated with keeping a home and minding children to lay the groundwork for community as well as politics. Shelters in the format of group houses create an atmosphere of shared space and shared lives, as well as shared responsibilities. Consider a plantation, where new slaves, flung separately into an unknown and assumedly harsh environment cluster together, almost for safety, but certainly for security. Within the life cycle occur points of juxtaposition and separation, and the space a person occupies when they occur defines them. In other words, situations in which women find themselves in new groups or newly alone hold potential to create entirely new things, such as safety, security, learning, community. Laura Kaplan found this same link between literal space and political learning in her work with the underground abortion group Jane. She writes:

> There were unexpected consequences from using apartments for the abortions. Sometimes five women waited together in the living room. When the first woman came out of the bedroom, relieved and no longer pregnant, the tension in the room lessened. If she survived, then, most likely, each of them was going to survive. Whether they were teenagers or older married women, rich or poor, whatever their color, an instant camaraderie developed among them . . . counseling for an abortion was a time of crisis in a woman's life, when she was more open to new perspectives. [Jane] could use that opportunity as an educable moment to show her how her personal problems connected to a broader social picture. . . . If she questioned society's attitudes about abortion, she might begin to question much more. (1995, pp. 85, 87)

I would like to draw the floor plan of a shelter for you, walk with you through the spatial intimacy of dining rooms, living rooms, smoking rooms, and television rooms and share the natural groupings that occur in shelters, as they do in homes or dormitories: over food, situation comedies, cigarettes, and washing dishes. A resident who has returned to shelter speaks about how important these connections were to her:

> *When I first came through here I had no self-esteem. I didn't care about a thing. They helped to build my self-esteem up. Gave me clothes to wear, make myself care. You know when you come through these doors and things that you've been through it seems like you're nothing. And all it takes is for them to make you feel good inside and sometimes on the outside and that helps you get back up. And that's what they did to me. They gave me clothes to put on which they didn't have to. This one girl would always do my hair for me every week, every week, every Saturday or Sunday night she would do my hair for school and working. And that made me feel good to be able to walk out of the shelter with decent clothes on, my hair done and my head held up high. I was trying to do something. That made me feel real good.*

This is the aspect of shelter that women unknowingly fear will be absent; they speak of fearing long rows of cots and barren spaces but mean that they fear being so far from a home space that they know and recognize as their own. Picture too the bunk beds that shelters use to make space for more women, more children—bunk beds that create yet another shared space. This is difficult shared space, radical shared space, spaces in which it is hard to be alone, and spaces in which it is hard not to find someone who will listen or who needs to be listened to. Shared space provides tangible interpersonal outcomes: women make friends. In many cases, these women are alone or have small, rather than large, support networks. Often women in shelter realize that their old networks are insufficient. One resident, afraid of being alone once she leaves shelter, told us that:

> *Res.:*   *I've made friends here. They already said they'd help me with moving, and keep me company or visit me on holidays and stuff.*
> *Int.:*   *Do you think that's true?*
> *Res.:*   *Yeah.*
> *Int.:*   *Is that enough?*
> *Res.:*   *Yeah, it's enough.*

Women befriend one another in shelter, sharing skills, knowledge, laughter, and a lot of tears. This pattern is most clearly seen in more established residents; once comfortable in shelter, women seem to speak more and reach out to the other residents.

> Int.: *Have you talked to anybody here about the kinds of things that went on between you and your abuser?*
>
> Res.: *Yes . . . I think my most support comes from the other women. We talk a lot because we can relate to [each other's situations]. Sometimes [we talk over] dinner or just sitting in the living room. They smoke cigarettes, and we just . . . start talking and we'll start playing spades. It always comes out.*

Space does not automatically convert into friendship. Despite sharing space, women choose to keep or break their silence and to share or retain their privacy. As Abu-Lughod writes, in reference to Awlad 'Ali society, "Members of a residential community do not choose to live with one another but are thrown together . . . " (1995, p. 26). The relationships formed in shelter, then, are deliberate acts. Honig reminds us that groups of women, which she calls sisterhoods, "may as easily confirm and perpetuate traditional social relationships as challenge them" (1995, p. 60). Yet these relationships are foundational to women's shelter experiences, and in some cases the friendships may even undermine the shelter's intent. Former residents provide the perspective of just how important the mix of other women in shelter was to their experience. For one resident, the women she met in shelter are now her friends and support network as she moves on:

> Int.: *So it sounds like it really makes a difference who else is in shelter with you.*
>
> Res: *Well, see, now like them I keep in touch with is [another resident] I keep in touch with [another resident]. Those are the only two I keep in touch with,—and—And basically, I talk to—four and five times a day. Cuz she lives out here by me.*

For many former residents, the other women in shelter provided the catalyst to draw them out, in order to help them with their troubles and in so doing forget some of their own. Ironically, this is one variable over which shelters have little if any control. However, it is clear that these shelters foster relationships by supporting and in some cases mandating constant interaction among the women in the house via house meetings, support group meetings, transitional meetings, and the chore system (for instance, this fosters women eating meals together). These relationships also are important between residents and staff. In the Furies collective, women found that "personal bonds need to precede the obviously political" (Rita Mae Brown, 1995, p. 131) while in other groups, friendships were pivotal to the ability to even begin political conversations (Honig, 1995, p. 71). The framework for these friendships, both between residents and staff, is laid from the very first time a woman walks through the shelter door.

Through the Shelter Door

Women enter shelter for many reasons; most center on the fact that there is, literally, nowhere else to go. Shelters are a "last resort," the place you call when you have no other options. Such women's outlook is understandably bleak, and their expectations for shelter are low; many want only a thin lifeline to keep them from plunging from the precipice. Education is not on their agenda.

Some women come from their own homes; others come from families and friends, endangered by their presence. Still others come from the streets:

> *Well, anyway, [my child and I went to see] about [services for the homeless] because we had been sleeping on the street and the policeman come. And so I went down there to register and they told me about [shelter]. I didn't get in that day. I didn't get in until like two weeks later, after my abuser had found me and [my son] in the street and he beat me. It was during the night and we hid under the bushes away from him. And the next morning, I went back to [the homeless agency] and that's when I got into [shelter].*

Shelter is the last place most women want to be—with the exception of home with their abuser.[1]

Women who come to domestic violence shelters often express surprise by what they find, due in large part to the fact that domestic violence shelters are quite different from their other shelter counterparts, whether for homeless people, food kitchens, or Red Cross–aided disasters. Women and children come as refugees to a war camp, and find community. Their mental picture is one of a cold-night shelter—or slave quarters—with no privacy, no belongings, little to eat and abandonment the next morning to the streets. The description of their expectations is educationally important; learning occurs *in context*. These women, entering shelter, expect the worst, and their relief is palpable:

> *Int.:* *What was your idea in your head of what a shelter would be like?*
> *Res.:* *Exactly that—shelter.*

---

1. Use of the phrase, "their abuser," or "her abuser," is controversial, as it identifies women with their abusers. However, a better phrase has not yet emerged from the literature, and to avoid awkwardness (e.g., "the man who battered her," or "the man who abused her"), I have regrettably used the shorter phrase.

Int.:   *What did it look like?*

Res.:   *I didn't think it [would] look as good as my house. I really
          didn't think it was gonna be this comfortable inside really. And
          I said oh Gosh they're gonna be all old and creepy in here and
          probably church music playing or something.*

Int.:   *Okay.*

Res.:   *You know how it is like when . . . Well I don't want to use that
          as an example. I was gonna say like a preacher's house or
          something but you know, refrained. I didn't think it was gonna
          be. . . . This place in my head I had no idea they would have
          something like this. And my 10-year-old seen this and said all
          right. And there was a Barney doll somewhere around here, I
          don't know where that's at but he fell in love with the Barney
          doll. I mean gosh he loves Barney.*

Other residents are even more straightforward:

*Well I imagined one big room where you put your cots up and you
take folding tables out. I didn't know what to expect. So I saw that
they had private rooms and [a] little dining room and a kitchen
and everybody cooks and everybody cleans. So I saw that it was
workable. And they said 'are you going to bring your things in?'
And I said 'I don't know yet. Let me finish looking around.' But
she made me feel pretty good. I think at that point I was still thinking that I wanted to go home. I was still feeling that way until
about two weeks after I got here.*

*Ultimate fear. I was so scared. I knew I wasn't gonna come. The
idea about coming to a shelter you know the horror stories you
hear about shelters and then there had recently been a movie on
TV about a homeless family and the places they had been and I
just, I was terrified. I really was scared.*

These women found that the shelters they entered were different than they
feared. They found independence and homes instead of subservience and
destitution, and the potential for intimacy where anonymity was expected.

Settling in to Shelter Life

Entering shelter is in itself liberatory; as Marilyn Frye argues, "Such a denial
of access [by women, to men] is also to claim the power of naming for one-
self: 'The slave who excludes the master from her hut thereby declares herself *not a slave*' " (in Hoagland, 1995, p. 280, emphasis in original).

However, defining what one is not is not quite the same as deciding what one is, or will be. Women entering shelter often are disoriented. They have received the shelter phone number from someone concerned—sometimes a friend, but more often a social worker, minister, health care worker, or police officer. Shelter is not an option women willingly choose; it is an option women exercise because they need help. One new resident tells us she came to shelter not for herself but because of her children:

> *Well this girl out here she just kept saying to me . . . you need this for you and your kids you know you really don't have nowhere else to go. And then she said you're gonna end up going back with him and I was. I really was. I was gonna go back. I really was. And regardless you know. She said that's abuse you know. How you gonna keep taking that abuse time and time again. And she said you know you really make me mad after all I try to look out for you and all. So I had to listen to her and I say yes she was right. You know I really didn't want to do that. Because I just feel this is so embarrassing you know. Like I really set myself up for that, so I was so embarrassed you know. And then when you gotta go around and tell everybody you know well this happened.*

When a woman admits she is being abused, she also is confessing to any number of other things: admitting her parents were right about the boyfriend, husband, or partner; admitting that she needs help; admitting that she can't "fix" the situation through her own efforts. Imagine the feeling of making your troubles public—in a society where domestic violence is still viewed both by its victims and by the larger society, as an individual problem—without a solution. Often, it is the realization that children are becoming secondary victims of the violence, either by viewing or by becoming abused themselves, that prompts women to enter shelter. It is a critical and difficult decision, prompted by the fundamental need for safety.

CHAPTER 3

(Re)gaining Consciousness

You got a right, I got a right
We all got a right to the tree of life
Yes, the tree of life.
—*You Got a Right*, African-American spiritual

The process of moving into and living in shelter changes women; sometimes, those who begin silently, find their voice. Others become listeners, creating community with other women who share their fate. But women share the disorientation, the fears, and the relief of finding that shelter is both more than they expected and demands more of them than many anticipated.

After residents "settle in" to shelter life, changes often take place. One of the first observable changes frequently involves the ability to verbalize their experiences of abuse. As one resident recounts,

Res.: *At first I wouldn't talk. I would not talk. The only person I would talk to is [one staff member], because that's the only one I trusted. Because that's the one I remembered from my first stay. That's the only person I would talk to. I was upset. They'll tell you I kept saying at every meeting I was forced to come here.*

Int.: *So what changed that you started to talk. Or did you?*

Res.: *I did, I think because I started meeting more women. And I started listening to the other women, I started trusting the other women.*

This resident's story points out her newly acquired voice, and the beginnings of community and education. The silencing of battered women is nearly constant, nearly impermeable, nearly suffocating. It is so much a part of women's lives that when they enter shelter, their instincts maintain their silence: no one has listened to them in so long, including family members, friends, and children. Their silence feels, if not natural, then self-protective.

27

In a reversal of Audre Lorde's phrase, these women have learned that, to some extent, their silence *will* protect them. Of course this protection has finite limits, and these limits are what has driven them, in large part, to shelter.

Among the drawbacks to women's silence is that violence becomes abstract to the rest of society, and therefore less painful; we see it in numeric terms rather than names and faces. The National Coalition of Violence Against Women is currently collecting names of women killed by their abusers for their project, "Remember my Name." Like the AIDS quilt and the Clothesline Project, they hope to pin a human face on tragedy. Someone has written that statistics are people with the tears wiped off. In person, the realities of violence become inescapable. Women arrive in shelter often without clothing or personal belongings; they do, however, carry the baggage of their stories.

I need to introduce you to the youngest woman/girl we interviewed for this research. "Nina" is 18 and in high school. Her words even now leap off the page. Ruth Behar might include her story in her category of "anthropology that breaks your heart" (Behar 1997). Her story, which is true, is "just" a statistic; a single woman with an abusive boyfriend. She entered shelter with this story:

> *I had an argument with my boyfriend and he had been drinking and I didn't come here the very first night that it happened, I came like the next day. He messed me up. He was mad because I didn't want to get close to him because he had been drinking. He likes to drink a lot and back then I was supposed to go get some training for a job but during school so then I told him that I was coming home about 9:30 but what happened was one of the speakers did not arrive and we got out early so I went home. He came at 5:30 and stayed until 6:30 and he thought I was still in school at the time so he started arguing with the security guard because he thought the security guard was covering up for me. He finally came home around 11:00 or 12:00 really drunk and he said "Where were you, I was looking for you and you wasn't here and you weren't there and didn't I tell you that I was coming at 5:30?" He was smelling really bad. You know where he was sleeping tonight because he usually sleeps on the couch when he drinks and we got into this big argument. He wanted to get close to me and . . . He grabbed me ugly, . . . and we had a visitor from New York, his friend. And he was kicking me because I didn't want to get close to him so then I fell off of the bed and I said all right fine, go to your bed . . . go ahead . . . and I was like "That's wrong what you did." I got up*

and I was going to go sleep in the bathroom so that we wouldn't fight anymore and when I got up to go he grabbed me by my arm and I said "Let go." He said, "You are going to sleep in the bathroom?" I said, "Yeah." Then he started arguing and he also was twisting my arm. Then I got loose and he grabbed me by my butt and started squeezing me by my butt and at that time I started getting upset and so it was the first time that I fought him back. And he was like shocked and I was like I don't know where I got my strength and I [was] just holding him down and pulling him on the floor. And I . . . where did all of my strength came or whatever. Then, his friend woke up. He said, "Man, are you gonna let her do that to you. You supposed be kicking her ass, she not supposed to be doing that to you." So then he dragged me to the bathroom and his friend wanted to get in it too so his friend kept trying to come into the bathroom and I was flinging and everything and his parents were there too. They were in the other room because it was like everybody had come to . . . and everybody was like drunk in the house except for his mother and they thought that their son did too much fighting. They would just laugh and said that they [are] having lovers fights. Let them go through whatever they want to. He dragged me in the bathroom and started holding me up by my hair and I told him to let go and he wouldn't let go. Then he finally did let go, his hands came from my head and instead of going he started choking me. It was like he was choking me real hard and I couldn't breathe anymore. At that time, at that point I was just like, "You know, you are going to keep doing this to me. You might as well just kill me now because I just can't take anymore. My body can't take anymore because he is always doing this to me for certain stuff. And I have been a good girl to him, I haven't cheated on him, I have been real good. I come straight home. I did everything for him and I . . . so he is choking me. And I was at my last breath and just said God please take my soul. And everything just stopped. He let go. Because I guess he knew that if he held me any longer I would die. He said, "get up." Get up and I couldn't get up because I was crying and I couldn't breathe. I have asthma and I couldn't breathe at all. He took off all of my clothes and threw them in the bathtub and he told me if you don't get up I am going to stomp you. And he turned on the cold water and I was trying to get out of the tub and he kept pushing me in the water. We started arguing. He told me if you be good, you stop crying I am going to put the hot water on and you won't be cold anymore. He put it on for a little while but I couldn't control my crying so he

*put the cold water on again. And then he kept pushing me in the
water and I couldn't breathe and I was crying and finally I just,
when he was trying to change the water I just jumped out of the
tub and started . . . and he goes "I am going to stop, I'm going to
stop beating you but you have to go on the bed, lie down, and not
talk and hug me and kiss me and do whatever I tell you to do. And
what's going to happen to you, what's going to happen to you if
you try to leave me?" "You're going to beat me." "What I can't
hear you?" "You're going to beat me." "And what else." "If you
leave me what is going to happen?" "You're going to find me and
kill me." "I can't hear you." I had to keep saying that until I got it
right. Then I went to lie down. I was close to him but not real close
to him and then he pulled me by [my] hair to come close to him to
sleep with him and he said to "do me like you love me." So I just
slept and didn't ever say anything after that. The next morning he
was messing with me. "Give me a kiss. Give me my lucky kiss for
the day. You come straight from school after that thing." And I
always thought that because he was going out for a while and I . . .
my teachers and everybody and my friends, the friends that I do
have because he wouldn't let [me] have but a few friends. . . . I
always pretended that nothing was going on and so I just couldn't
take any more. . . . It started out with pushing me and then yelling
at me for simple things. And then he wouldn't talk to me for days.
He would be mad about something but he wouldn't tell me. He
would just be mad and stop talking to me. And I used to cry for
that. Because I was like what did I do and I couldn't think of anything I had did. After that he started pulling my hair a lot and
telling me, don't you move from that spot. If you move from that
spot I am going to kick your ass. And let's say that I am sitting
right here and watching TV and I want to get up to go to the bathroom, you ask me permission to get up. "Can I go to the bathroom?" "No." "Please let me go." "You got five minutes." Then if
I didn't come back in five minutes he would come in the bathroom, unlock the door, and take me from the bathroom, whatever
I am doing and put me back . . . and then he would said don't even
move. So I would just stay there. I wouldn't move because he
would drag me from wherever I want to go and at night he has
feelings that he is a light sleeper. So anytime you move he'll get up
and be like "what you doing?" Sometimes I am just going to the
bathroom or getting me a drink of water and one night I was like
I'm going to the bathroom but I go to the kitchen. He got up, "I
knew you wasn't going to the bathroom. What are you doing in*

the kitchen?" I told him I got thirsty. "But didn't you tell me you were going to the bathroom." And I was just like, "Yes." And I got my ass kicked so bad and he had pinned me on the bed. We had a big argument. "You go where I tell you to go. You want to go here, you want to go there, you ask permission." I couldn't understand. And we had already started living together. After he got out of jail we started living together and that was a big mistake. He just started trying to control me, everything I did, everybody I spoke to. I couldn't talk to my girlfriends or to my cousins. Because he said they all are whores. He said, "you want to hang out with whores, those girls they look like hookers. That's what they look like. You want to be with them hanging right there, everybody is going to think that my girl is a hooker." So then one day he embarrassed [me] so bad that I was talking to my friend. He came up and said, "I told you, why are you talking [to] this hooker?" In front of my friends, and I was so embarrassed. And all of my girlfriends were pissed off. And from that day they said you had better leave him. Don't let him control you. He said, "If I see you talking to them, I'm going to kick your ass when you get home."

It was amazing to us that Nina spoke so freely. In part, she got out "early." The enduring silences we found emanated from women who had been abused for long periods of time—but often beginning, like Nina, very early.

Nina chose this particular shelter because of a voice on the phone that sounded caring. After very little care in her life, Nina wanted to escape—but not to an environment that might remind her of the life she had lived. She, like other women, responded to the hope of something better and a place where they might tell their stories and move beyond them. As she tells it, without that one voice she would not have left her abusive boyfriend:

We had called other hotlines then when we got through to here the person was so compassionate. You could just tell by her voice. Other people sounded like they just didn't want to be bothered and then, I don't know. . . . They were like, "come to this place" and I called and then they were like "Yo, well what's your problem" and all of this. And I was like why would I want to go someplace like that. If I wanted to be talked to like that I would go home. Because my boy, he would talk to me like that. So they said . . . so we started looking more and called a few more different ones. They weren't really nice so I just said never mind I don't want to go into there. I would just go home. Then they would say "come on let's do it just one more time" and so they finally said,

"You know I talked to this lady that sounded really nice. And I called and talked to and she was really nice. She had something different that the other people. . . . Other people were like, you know, . . . so go. If [this shelter worker] was like the other people on the phone then I would not have ever left home. I would have still been with him.

Shelters are fragile places, full of women like Nina who have come on the slim hope of finding someone to care enough to listen.

Telling Stories

I have not told you Nina's story to shock, although it does. I have told it in illustration of how some of these women's stories come rushing out, like a torrent of water long frozen in the winter of their silence. They are unstoppable and heartbreaking. Lockwood (1996) writes about the importance of the stories we tell, referring to stories with the power of truth (as in these women telling the truths about their lives to one another) that have the power to create new ways of understanding.

Shelters structure both private and public opportunities for such stories. Let me ground this in an understanding of how shelters operate, beginning with the public side. Most shelters, if not all, have particular requirements that women must fulfill. In some cases, women must file for a restraining order, also known as a civil protection order. In others, requirements may include seeking housing, child care, or formal education. In general, the process follows a pattern: a woman enters shelter, in itself an overwhelming experience. She is often fed and clothed, and given the chance to tell her story then—for the first time. Then the requirements must be met: in Washington, D.C., a woman must report to the office in charge of homelessness within 24 hours of entering shelter in order to receive food stamps, Aid to Families with Dependent Children (AFDC), or other forms of federal and local support. There, she must tell her story again, at least in part, to be allowed to remain in shelter. This chain continues: a civil protection order or restraining order requires, again, that a woman tell her story. That she appear in court. That she acknowledge, publicly, her private trauma.

An immediate reaction to such requirements, and a valid one, is that the women are victimized again, and that this is unnecessarily cruel to a fragile population. However, the women I spoke with talked of this frenzy of activity as both overwhelming and as forcing the women to take control back over their lives. Activist Angela Miles has also expressed this. As Gere Lewis summarizes,

> Within the frames of phallic discourse, speaking the stories of our abuse, violation, poverty, marginalization, and powerlessness—

and these in their varied cadences across different cultural, historical, class, race, and sexual identities—requires not the voice of a
victim but that of a powerful sense of a self refusing to be subordi-
nated. (1993, p. 21)

Shelters deliberately structure these opportunities, forcing women to confront their own subordination; at My Sister's Place, one of the shelters that
participated in this research, this policy is expressed as empowerment. Their
credo recognizes that shelter residents must be in control of their own lives,
and that power over their decisions, long denied them, must be returned at
all costs. Their mission states this premise: *MSP is an interactive community
committed to eradicating domestic violence. It provides safe, confidential
shelter, programs, education, and advocacy for battered women and their
children. The overarching goal is to empower women to take control of
their own lives.* Or, in the words of one resident:

> *When I came, I realized if I want to help myself, they were willing
> to help me—because if you don't want to help yourself, you won't
> get nowhere.*

I use this shelter as an example of many women's shelters, across the country, which similarly tie together voice, empowerment, and women's survival.[1]

Public storytelling also represents a taking back of one's own experiences, of reframing them for a purpose: to get help, to evoke sympathy, to
elicit understanding—even to shock. Even when it is not successful, these
women gain the power of being able to talk back, to tell their side of the
story. The following narrative relates an incident where a battered women
took on police officers, and the courts.

> Res.: *Over the last 14 months I called the cops five times. Of those
> five times I was arrested four times. Of the four times, three
> times I should have been in a hospital cause I was hurt that
> bad. And the one time we didn't get arrested they laughed at
> the situation. They thought it was funny.*
> Int.: *Did you both get arrested?*
> Res.: *Yes. One time he didn't, only I did. 'Cause I was talking. I was
> trying to get him out of there and um and they said, "Ms. ——
> did you scratch your husband's neck ?" and I said "yes, 'cause
> he was choking me and it was the only thing I could get to."*

---

1. Again, this work specifically references two shelters. However, in conversations with a
   number of other shelters, shelter workers, formerly battered women, and women's advocates, it seems that a number of shelters follow this framework.

> *And they said, "remove your jewelry" and he said "see that's what you get for opening your mouth."*
>
> Res.: *And he walked out of the room and they arrested me, they didn't arrest him. That was the one time that he didn't get arrested. The other times he was arrested also and then when they "note paper" it they release you at the same time to go home together. With no regard what may happen on the way home, once you're home, the next day, the next year. You know there's ... the system is bad.*

This incident highlights an unsuccessful public storytelling, as well as a true example of the lack of assistance police offer in domestic violence situations. Nonetheless, she remains glad that she spoke out. For her, this incident occurred early in a long series of lessons in learning to speak out, loudly and long, for her rights and those of her children.

The private telling takes on a different tone. It can be less belligerent, although not always. It is inevitably sadder, both because women recognize themselves in each other's stories and because as they see themselves in each other, they begin to see that their stories are not unique but are those of a people, a nation, of women.

Storytelling serves as the epicenter of shelter teaching and learning. As such it encompasses a process that goes beyond therapy, or as Magda Gere Lewis writes,

> The importance of the feminist focus on 'the story' born of experience is not the vacuous and gratuitous telling of our private stories as a cathartic moment, but, indeed, to emphasize that subordinate groups live subordination and marginality through our subjectivity, that we live it through social relations which are inscribed in personal practices which are, in turn, reflective and constitutive of our social organization. It is to emphasize that our subordinations are lived precisely in the context of the details of our individual experiences which, to the extent that they can be made to seem to be private, cannot then offer the ground for a collective political practice. (1993, pp. 9–10)

Her words should evoke the pedagogy of consciousness-raising that arose in the 1970s as "activist and politically committed women came to apply the universal demands for equality and justice of the civil rights movement to their own situation as women" (Weiler 1988, p. 125; see also bell hooks 1981, 1984).

Raising Consciousness and Raising Hell

These first consciousness-raising groups often were led by women who were already politicized in some ways and were actively engaging in translating politics to their own lives. Hence the phrase, evocative of the personal items women inscribed with political messages (see chapter 2), emerged: the personal is political. Consciousness-raising (CR) in shelters takes a different form, although maintaining the centrality of the personal in politics. Consciousness means the very way in which reality is constructed and accepted. CR creates a new awareness and sensitivity to women, as well as the way women's lives are structured by society (Sheila 1973). Most important for the domestic violence agenda, women's prior acceptance of their place or treatment in life becomes problematic. Of course, this process is neither simple nor quick: as Adrienne Rich reminds us,

> The awakening of consciousness is not like the crossing of a frontier—one step and you are in another country.

CR also involves a very intense emotional component. Such personal sharing cannot be accomplished without this emotion, and it also contributes to social integration by creating shared social facts. Hyde (1986) describes the emotions that accompany CR as a form of "bonding":

> Women stressed the importance of bonding, of people getting to know each other so that they could work together in a way that was mutually fulfilling and rewarding. . . . Not only does the acknowledgment of emotions and bonding help people become invested, it also serves as a source of reserve energy in the face of opposition. Knowing that others care often comforts an individual when confronted with derogatory comments, hecklers, etc. Fears and concerns can be addressed within a supportive environment. This sounds obvious, yet it is often overlooked because accomplishing the task has assumed a disproportionate emphasis, to the detriment of the group. (p. 554)

Historically, consciousness-raising (Ruth 1973) is a method originally developed by women to educate each other about oppression. Its history extends back to Susan B. Anthony and the early women activists before the women's movement as such existed, and arguably in subtler terms in women's groups such as quilting circles. This continues today in many groups who feel that its ongoing practice is necessary (Brown 1992). It involves exchanging experiences in a small-group setting, which builds cohesion among women in a group and also heightens awareness to the problems that women *qua* women face. In the words of Robin Morgan

(1970), "the personal meaning of being a woman was redefined in political terms." Women's basic oppression-based problems such as sexual harassment, inequitable pay, and individual relationships, including domestic violence, were the focus of discussion during these group meetings, held in homes, churches, women's health clinics, or wherever safe space for women was available. According to Baker and Snodgrass (1979), groups regularized discussions of personal topics to reveal their larger political dimensions:

> Most consciousness-raising groups follow a format of selected topics and adopt a set of rules that structure interaction. Topics include sex-role socialization, the sexual division of labor (in marriage, childcare, and work outside the home), sexuality, and crimes against women such as rape and battering. (p. 260)

Sharing such personal stories created a kind of community among women, facilitated by the safety of CR spaces.

Consciousness-raising may well be the clearest example of feminist, political education in shelters. Of course, CR in the 1990s is not unique to shelters; its techniques have also been incorporated into a new form of pedagogy, which characterizes many women's studies classes today (Middleton 1993) as well as other organizations. The techniques followed vary from CR group to group, but the purpose and general format is the same. The National Organization for Women holds CR on a yearly basis, stating:

> CR changes people. It shakes us up and shows us new ways of looking at ourselves and our world. . . . Politics in this context refers . . . to the concept of power in society—who has it, how is it used, how one gets it, how society is managed. 'Political' means the web of relationships between an individual and society. When a woman recognizes that she has been conditioned to think her 'feminine' hands are clever enough for sewing and typing but not for surgery, she makes a political recognition. In CR we learn at a gut level that there are NO personal solutions to social problems— only adjustments, accommodations, temporary loopholes and pain. Changing society into a nonsexist community of women and men working equitably together is the only real solution to the basic problems women face. (January 1992, newsletter)

Consciousness-raising in Shelters

Consciousness-raising translates to the most basic details of shelter life, both overt and subtle. The most overt means of furthering feminist education in shelters is through deliberate consciousness-raising groups similar to those just discussed. According to Klein (1984), role conflict leads women to become involved in the feminist social movement because they develop a feminist consciousness, defined as "a recognition of women as a group, an understanding of problems as public rather than personal (p. 3). However, the shelter setting again provides a different perspective. Women in shelters are not limited to *role* conflict; they have actual, *physical* conflict [There is a clear link between the two; it is the men's sexist roles in society and the powers those roles convey that form the foundation for physical, emotional, and sexual abuse]. This in essence summarizes a key distinction in feminist pedagogy at universities and that at these shelters: at universities, faculty struggle to legitimate the use of experience as knowledge (c.f. Magda Gere Lewis 1993; Maher and Tretrault 1994; Ropers-Huilman 1998), while in shelters, there is literally nowhere else to start. Theory bubbles below the surface for shelter workers, but for battered women, their experiences are preeminent. They express impatience with theory, feeling that it disembodies their experiences and fails to represent their lives. Battered women are in shelter explicitly because of their experiences and lack the luxury of theory. bell hooks remarks that "the academic setting, the academic discourse . . . is not a known site for truthtelling" (1989, p. 29). Shelters, in contrast, must be such sites. Thus, the struggle for shelter workers is not to remain limited to experience but to join women's experiences together in such a way that commonalities, and then theory, become self-evident.

Formerly battered women who enter shelter generally are not politicized about gender-based oppression, although they may be about racism, the politics of disability, or citizenship. Shelters deliberately structure consciousness-raising through support groups, physical structure (e.g., dormitory-style living arrangements), and by placing women with stories in common together. In the two shelters I studied, women were required to attend a number of meetings during the weekday evenings; within semistructured groups, women found both safety and dialogue. The primary consciousness-raising group, by whatever name, generally consisted of a facilitator (in some cases, a social worker; in others, a volunteer or a formerly battered woman, some of whom were on staff at both shelters) and all the adult residents of the shelter. In a closed-door session (i.e., no other staff), women would be invited to tell their stories around a central theme (e.g., the honeymoon phase of the cycle of violence). In some instances, the theme was introduced first; in others, the theme arose from the women (e.g., "it was just like a honeymoon!"), at which point a staffer might interject the theme; in still others, the theme emerged in the middle or at the end. Regardless, the central focus was the women's stories—what was the same, what was different, what did one do, how did it work out, what did they learn? Tears are here, as well:

> *We had a meeting yesterday. Like a support group and I was cry-ing. The new girl Sarah was crying too. Everybody was crying. This is a good group. We had listened to this song by Karen White about being alone. I would rather be alone than to stay here . . . and you know there are times that you feel that it is not right why do you have to be in love . . . why stay and be in love and not be happy at all. If I am unhappy with you and without you I might as well be [by] myself. So that was what the song was about. I started crying first because I had just come from court. So I was already strung up anyway and when I came home . . . I wasn't trying to talk to anybody but then we had a meeting so I was trying to be quiet and keep my emotions to myself and then all of sudden (cry-ing) everybody was like so supportive. All the girls were there and we had a good talk and it's like you feel lighter afterward. There is all of the girls there like "yeah girl I know what you talking about," "exactly" and everybody started crying after that. Then you say something else "Yeah" and then instead of crying you end up laughing because it's like just the way everybody is.*

This is precisely the way in which Catherine MacKinnon defines "the per-sonal is political":

> women's distinctive experience as women occurs within that sphere that has been social lived as the personal—private, emo-tional, interiorized, particular, individual, intimate—so that, what is to know the politics of women's situation is to know women's personal lives." (1983, p. 247)

In some ways, shelter-based CR groups, because they are more struc-tured than many other shelter activities, are thus more readily identified as pedagogical. For example, shelter groups use a loosely defined curriculum. The content is seemingly straightforward and overtly political: topics in shelter discussions include the cycle of violence, safety planning, sexism in society, recognizing signs of a batterer, and other pertinent topics. Yet the content is not "delivered," per se; if it begins as a one-way exchange, this is not the case for long. Instead, the mention of the cycle of violence, for exam-ple, tends to elicit women's stories of their own experiences—that is, the group becomes a space where "students fashion their voices" (Maher and Tretrault 1994). Therefore, support groups feature interactive and some-times indistinguishable content and process dimensions.

I have drawn diagrams of the cycle of violence for and with shelter personnel, knowing that they would be used only cursorily to explain the actual cycle, and that more often than not the outcome of the discussion would be women's stories about their own experiences of the three phases: honeymoon, tension-building, and acute battering incident. This is painful learning for women, and painful listening for shelter workers. Consider the honeymoon phase of battering. In this phase, an abuser is apologetic. He can bring flowers, candy, dinner. It is the Valentine's Day of which dreams are made. He promises, "never again." He makes excuses for his behavior and declares his love. He is caring, considerate, the man she thought she married/decided to live with/began dating. How much more attractive it is to believe this story than the one in which she ends up on the floor, bleeding. At the hospital, with a broken limb. At the shelter, where she is disconnected from him, above all:

> *Then that night he kept calling me, and calling me and saying he was sorry and everything and he would never, ever put his hands on me again. "I swear baby never again." And then that Friday he got locked up again for another drug charge. So I waited for him. I felt that I should not leave him right now because he just got locked up and he said that he was never going to do it again and everything. And I said that this was a bad time to leave him while he was going to jail.*

These experiences can be too painful even to acknowledge outside of the support group. One resident refused to discuss the groups at all, as though they did not exist. Other residents, who felt they could be more open, pointed out the power of these groups, as the following quotes illustrate.

> *Those groups helped a lot because ...you always think you're the only one that goes through things and you sit around and listen to these other women and think.*

Int.: *What have you learned about domestic violence even listening to these women talk to you.*

Res.: *That it's really out there. It's really out there, you know. And even one [woman in] our support group when she's talking I thought, god, I thought my [situation] seemed bad now yours is worse. I mean and the girls that had left him had knocked their teeth out and this and that. I'm like oh my god. I didn't have it that bad but I thought it was embarrassing and wouldn't show it off outside but . . . I don't know.*

These meetings, variously titled "house," "group," "parenting," or other unrevealing terms, ostensibly dealt with a number of separate issues, such as chores around the house, proper ways to discipline children, and house rules and regulations, as well as topics specifically related to domestic violence. Inevitably, however, these meetings—whether targeted toward an explicit examination of the dynamics of domestic violence or not—seemed to turn toward group-based explorations of oppression based on women's life experiences. I do not mean to imply that all meetings, all groups, all gatherings at shelters fully accomplish the goals of consciousness-raising, only that once introduced to the idea of building a collective story, shelter residents found numerous opportunities to continue such a conversation. Frequently, as a result of CR in a shelter setting, women realize that the violence they have experienced is not only not their fault, but is related to violence in society rather than being unique to their lives—a realization sparked by the similarity of stories told by woman after woman. Or, in the words of Audre Lorde,

> As we begin to recognize our deepest feelings, we begin to give up, of necessity, being satisfied with suffering and self-negation, and with the numbness which so often seems like their only alternative in society. Our acts against oppression become integral with self, motivated and empowered from within. (1981, p. 58)

These groups deliberately infuse feminist theory:

> *Staff:* *How much gender inequality affects their lives, first of all. I mean, that's the feminist piece of what we're doing and that's the unique piece of what we're doing that's different, I think what a lot of other programs that are teaching, [is] life skills and this and that.*
>
> *But teaching them not just gender inequality but oppression in general, how a lot of the problems quote/unquote that they have or the issues that they've had to deal with are not their own individual issues, they're not because of their own life, you know. Class issues, race issues—all those things—I hope that when people come through our doors, they're going to get politicized, you know. But the people are going to understand the effects that the larger society have and the role that the larger society plays in their lives to be a big part of the reason for a lot of the—their approach to things and a lot of the reason for how they came to be where they are today.*

But at the same time, not to use that as a convenient excuse, but to use that . . . along with their own steps that they've taken and their own responsibility that they have to take for their actions, but understanding to what extent they've acted based on socialization and that's what I try to teach. And you know that when you walk through the door the medium is the message. It's a house full of women. A lot of women are taught from the beginning that if you don't have a man in your environment, it's a useless place to be, it's futile, it's a terrible place to be.

I've had women tell me, you know, before I came here, I thought if there wasn't a man around, there was no reason to be around anywhere, a place, you know, maybe never experiencing sisterhood. [Shelter structure] is not an accident. Experiencing sisterhood is something a lot of people never experience because of the fact that—the divide and conquer thing, you know, we're going to be divided from each other and taught to compete with one another for men and so on and so forth and it goes on and on.

I . . . helping women to begin to trust other women, feel supported by other women, feel that they can support other women, to end this—at least chip away at the sort of inability that women have had for so long to help one another because they've been socialized against doing just that. We have a conspiracy of silence ending that. I mean, just how many women come in and their sisters and their mothers are less helpful to them and less supportive of them in their struggle than their brothers and their fathers sometimes.

And to begin to help them to be supportive of other women and understanding of other women and understanding of the common oppression that we share. And you know, you say "what do I want to teach." I don't teach that. I don't sit and teach that. What I do whenever I have the opportunity is facilitate a conversation between them so that they can begin to see, and here and there maybe say a sentence that's going to help them to frame what they're saying but they learn that from each other.

As a staffer describes, a great deal of their teaching is done by weaving women's stories together to gently nudge women toward learning from each other:

> Staff: You have a room full of women and they're talking about whatever, they're talking about the abuse they've suffered or how—let's say they're talking about mothers, families and how they've helped or not helped, the common threads. Mainly just by pointing out the common threads and asking questions. You know like "Hey, Tina and Jane and Samantha, you're all saying that your families weren't supportive. Isn't that kind of crazy? What does that mean?" You know, and "I've heard 50 million other women sit in this room and say exactly that. That doesn't make any sense. Why would all these families not be supportive. What's going on here; maybe we can understand where this comes from. Where do you think this comes from," you know.

Shelter consciousness-raising emphasizes women's common experiences of violence as critical bonds that women in shelter share.

Because workers also have stories to share, CR can also cross the boundary between residents and workers. As one shelter director revealed, her own experience with CR was pivotal:

> The raising of consciousness is a lifelong process which is gradual. It happens drop by drop, over the course of a lifetime. Nonetheless, there are some moments that can be viewed as turning points in the consciousness-raising process, and I want to share two of those with you.
>
> First, when I was just turning 20, I met a woman who was later to become my closest friend and mentor. We were both living in the Middle East at the time, and one day, we were chatting. I told her about another friend of mine who had a father who was working in Saudi Arabia for the year. This friend had wanted to visit her father in Saudi Arabia, but she could not go because no women are permitted to enter that country without a male escort, and she did not have one. Not only that, but women in that country are not permitted to have a bank account, own property, or even to drive a car!
>
> As I relayed all of this information about that country to my friend, she listened intently. I said something like, "Well, I sure am glad I don't live there!"

My friend said, "What difference does it make?" I said, "What do you mean?" She then explained. She told me that as long as any woman in the world is oppressed because she is a woman, then all women are oppressed.

This type of revelation is precisely the intent of consciousness-raising activities, whether conducted in domestic violence shelters or elsewhere.

CR above all welds together the shelter community. The strength of this community, in large part, determines the ability of individual women to survive the emotional upheaval of shelter life, through simultaneously politicizing women to reexamine where they place blame for their abuse (and credit for their escape) as well as ensuring that they are surrounded with supportive others.

Two aspects of domestic violence shelters seem to facilitate these kinds of events and interactions. The first of these, the proximity built into shelter space, simply provides opportunities to connect. As women become conversant with the shelter routine and structure, these conversations begin: in the smoking room, in the living room, in the safe space of consciousness-raising support groups, over dinner. Staff talk with residents, women talk with each other, mothers try to answer their children's questions about a "real" home and "daddy." Women begin to reveal the stories that they were embarrassed or ashamed to tell: stories of physical abuse, of sleepless nights, of fear, and loneliness, and love; stories of police reactions, of co-workers' discomfort, of depression, of sexual abuse, of isolation, of the men they love over and over again, the ways they'd tried to "fix" things. Trying to make sure the house was immaculate; the children were quiet; they were dressed well, polite to his friends, responsive to his needs, didn't "sass back" or act "uppity," didn't ask for money, or have friends, or fix green peas, or forget to iron a favorite shirt, or. . . . And as the stories meld together, women start to meet each other eye to eye, and shape their own realizations: it wasn't me. There was nothing I could have done. It really wasn't my fault.

The second, equally important dimension, is the value placed on women's stories and experiences, an important concept to feminist pedagogy in formal education environments as well. A third concept, central to informal educational environments, is the philosophy shared by these two shelters (and many others) that women know their own lives and should make their own decisions. That is, at the same time that shelters are asking women to tell, and retell, their stories, looking for connections with other women and examining the implications of their own choices, shelters also ask women to use their newly acquired knowledge to make additional choices about their lives (see chapter 5).

Shelters' attempts to develop women's consciousness extend beyond classic CR groups. For example, shelters often develop conscious-raising materials, for both women in shelter and the women that surround them—shelter workers, volunteers, and family and friends. In my bookstore wanderings I encountered *The Domestic Violence Survival Kit* at the Sisterhood Bookstore in California. It contains the following: *Next Time She'll Be Dead*, by Ann Jones; *Getting Free*, by Ginny NiCarthy; *Surviving Domestic Violence*, by the Los Angeles Commission on Assaults Against Women (LACAAW); several pamphlets on home security, victim's rights, LACAAW services, and self-defense; several strategy cards on survival, safety strategies, assault strategies, an escape plan checklist, and warning signs of a potential batterer; as well as a hotline magnet, a "call police" car sign, and a coupon for a free self-defense class. Some materials are overtly political (e.g., the relative power of men and women in society), while others are designed to educate women about their options. A significant proportion of the more subtle pedagogical practices encompass these materials made available to women, and there are other textual and pictorial references to gender-based politics and liberation in the shelter environment: posters of Women Who Dared and Rosie the Riveter, slogans against violence, career possibilities, posted job openings. In particular, the career possibilities and posted job openings convey the feminist educational theme of accessibility, often discussed theoretically in university settings but a reality in shelters.

This form of consciousness-raising is not unlike the early and contemporary work of the Boston Women's Health Collective (BWHC), who wrote *Our Bodies, Ourselves*. Their purpose in creating their book was to educate women about their own bodies so that women could own their health care and understand their options, rather than naively depending on the advice of their doctors, which they might not understand. Similar materials are created by other health collectives, and by battered women's shelters to train volunteers, community workers, and victim/survivors of domestic abuse (c.f. Avery 1995). In its own right, shelter information echoes the BWHC by facilitating women's access to knowledge, options, and their right to action. Feminist practice links this kind of education and activism, particularly fostering women's access to the kinds of information with which women can make informed choices about their lives.

A Storm in a Haven

Shelters, although safe, are not calm places. They are not all CR groups and bonding; instead, they are places in which doors slam, women cry, children scream, and the shrill ring of the telephone punctuates any moment of the day or night. Emotions swirl over these women, as they tell stories and listen to more. Consciousness-raising takes place over breakfast; over bus tokens to get to downtown offices or housing possibilities; and in its most structured way, during support groups that are held for the residents (This of itself is interesting—hooks writes that some professors equate safe spaces with quiet ones. Shelters are the antithesis of quiet.)

Each of us, I think, who works in a shelter wishes with all her heart that each story was unique, that each woman we help would be the last of her line, the last of the abused needing bandages, the last story in the newspaper, the last tearful voice in the night. Each of us knows this is not so, and this learning comes painfully, over time, working with woman after woman. For the women who are in shelter, however, this learning process must be abridged, so that they also may see the links between themselves and other women. They lack the luxury of time and longitudinal understanding.

In a shelter where I worked many years ago, a newspaper article titled *The Dance of Safety* was taped to an office door. What I remember best was the rituals it described, rituals that all women are taught they must do if they want to be safe. They will be familiar to you as well: carry your keys in your hand; walk with purpose; walk with a partner at night; be aware of your surroundings; and so on. The point of the article, and of CR in shelters, is threefold: first, that all women must fight to be free of violence; second, that all women are together in this struggle. The power of CR in shelters emerges when a woman recognizes that the boundary of her pain is not really bounded to her individual life. Third, no matter what we do, none of us is safe until we all are.

CHAPTER 4

Learning Without Teachers,
Teaching Without Books

> I will overcome
> I will overcome . . .
> Down in my heart
> I do believe
> I will overcome someday.
> —African-American spiritual

Shelters, like many informal learning environments, do not primarily consider their mission to be "education." In contrast, mission statements tend to be couched in language such as "empowering women," "providing shelter," and "assisting women." Shelters are comfortable with raising consciousness, but fail to name it pedagogy. To add to the confusion, this vision is consistent with ideas about informal education:

> Whether we are parents or specialist educators, we teach. . . .
> Some of the time we work with a clear objective in mind—perhaps
> linked to some broader plan e.g. around the development of reading. . . . These ways of working all entail learning, but informal
> education tends to be unpredictable—we do not know where it
> might lead. In conversation we have to catch the moment where
> we can say or do something to deepen people's thinking or to put
> themselves in touch with their feelings. (Informal Education
> Homepage 1998, unpaginated)

This chapter lays out that theme, which, after hooks's work, I call "education as the practice of freedom," as well as the ways in which it is practiced across these shelters. hooks writes,

> Urging all of us to open our minds and hearts so that we can know
> beyond the boundaries of what is acceptable, so that we can think
> and rethink, so that we can create new visions, I celebrate teaching

that enables transgressions—a movement against and beyond boundaries. It is that movement which makes education the practice of freedom. (1994, p. 12)

I think that bell hooks would find shelter education as "the practice of freedom," and that this is the link across the two shelters.

Key to such practice are elements central to these two shelters, particularly the presence of workers who are willing to learn at the same time they teach, to share their stories at the same time that they listen. Again, hooks writes:

When education is the practice of freedom, students are not the only ones who are asked to share, to confess. Engaged pedagogy does not seek simply to empower students. . . . Teachers grow, and are empowered by the process. That empowerment cannot happen if we refuse to be vulnerable while encouraging students to take risks. (1994, p. 21)

Shelter workers and faculty share self-revelation, and self-learning.

At the end of the class, I've really had the opportunity to think about my teaching. I think of different ways of teaching. . . . It's sort of a self-feeding thing that goes on because we have excellent graduate students . . . and they push us as teachers and they push our research and ask questions of that. So then the work that is done here in terms of teaching and research is different than it would have been. And it's a circle. (Ropers-Huilman, 1998, p. 99)

What is interesting to me is that in neither environment is this mutuality of teaching and learning expressed in a routine manner. Teachers do not evaluate students on the basis of what students have taught them or on the ways in which teachers' practice has or is changing on the basis of what they have learned from students.

This is an important contribution of Ropers-Huilman's study: that students and faculty are both teachers and learners. However, although the beliefs are enacted "[I] continually encouraged students to talk with and teach each other through class formats that included small group discussions, group projects, and class discussions" (1998, p. 99), I continue to believe that such relationships are implicit where they could, and often should, be made explicit. For example, in the shelter setting, women need to learn that they can depend on other women in their communities to assist them and how to form such mutually reinforcing relationships at a peer level. Likewise, students need to be guided to form such networks rather than depending on faculty members exclusively.

This last characteristic of the feminist pedagogy at these domestic violence shelters is, I believe, definitional of feminism itself. Feminism demands activism, and in this case it begins with the active learning of residents and the engagement of staff. In practice, this means a variety of things: staff listen actively, seeking opportunities to interject social commentary into women's stories about their lives. They actively participate in women's shelter lives, whether this entails eating meals with them, inquiring about their day, playing with their children, watching television or movies with them, or smoking a cigarette. They take a proactive stance toward women's learning.

At the same time, residents are pressed into taking similarly active stands toward their own learning in order to conform to shelter guidelines and expectations. Most women who stay in shelter for any length of time (longer than a week or two) seem to adapt well to this structure; as discussed earlier, this is not a one-size-fits-all approach.

Here I will also add a characteristic: shelter education expects no prior knowledge of domestic violence outside of her own experience, yet treats women respectfully. Let me say this another way. When a woman enters the shelter environment, there is nothing to signal that she should have known better, should have run faster, should have understood that the first violent contact would not be the last. In direct contrast, the shelter is set up in such a way that residents learn together, hearing their individual and collective patterns of abuse, and build an awareness together. At the same time, women are respected and praised, both by staff and other residents, for their skills and talents.

While shelters are not formally organized as educational spaces, learning nonetheless takes place. Shelters are, by definitions of informal education, learning environments. This distinction is important, as shelters in this text are revealed as spaces where teaching is done by women who define themselves as primarily other-than-teacher, and learning is done by women who define themselves primarily as other-than-student.

The terms *education* and *schooling* are often spoken in the same sentence or thought, and are as often confounded with one another. While schooling is commonly acknowledged as those learning processes and practices bounded by the formal school system, this boundary also often delimits our own research so that the larger context of education is often not considered. Our own definitions constrain us. Education is a constant process, structured by events as disparate as television, traveling to work, and interacting with other individuals. These effects, while sometimes considered in discrete forms such as studies on the effects of television on children, are not considered as part of a system of education almost entirely external to the formal system of schooling.

These informal or "nonformal" aspects—education outside the formal school system—are critical dimensions of two former studies I have recently undertaken that explicitly concern both education and schooling; however, education is the more important dimension of the two. This study is the third. All of these studies investigate particular *spaces* as educational environments. In this way, schools become one of many spaces that can be structured to deliver, enhance, or complement overt learning.

The first study concerned feminist teaching, and the limits and practice of feminist pedagogy. In part, I found that the practice of mentoring of new women faculty by established women faculty as feminist practice at the university. As part of a study of feminist teaching at the university level, conducted at multiple university campuses (both historically integrated and historically black), mentoring was found to be an important and meaningful part of the feminist responsibilities that women defined for themselves. However, this mentoring did not take place in any formalized way. It was neither part of the curriculum nor structured in an institutionalized sense. Few concepts cover learning that takes place outside of previously defined channels, and the literature indicates that most of these channels considered in any depth are located within the schooling paradigm. When we locate learning outside of the classroom, in a literal sense, we are forced to create or define the structure that houses and nurtures it (Sattler 1997).

This theme is echoed by the second study, which concerned the practices of informal science in federally funded grants, projects, and institutions. The nature of learning, whether by children or adults, is such that there are both formal and informal aspects—largely linked to the environment in which the learning is intended to occur. However, we know very little about the ways in which intended but informal learning is structured, and since it takes place in this case almost always, if not solely, outside of formal educational institutions there exists an entirely new and largely unexamined context for education. These other sites where education is both intended and takes place are part of the logical concept of lifelong learning, but they can also be considered as part of the larger educational context that frames schooling, as well as having structure and sequences of their own (Zantal-Wiener, Yin, and Sattler 1997).

In a similar manner, we may examine situations deliberately arranged for one purpose in terms of potential secondary purposes or effects; in this case, through the lens of education. Those gatherings where women politicize one another, such as quilting (see chapters 2, 5, and 7), are one historic example where both a primary activity—quilting—and many secondary activities—friendship, instruction in sewing technique, politicization, and education—take place.

These examples, and the remainder of this book, point out a political economy of education and educational research: there are some concepts that are seen as appropriate to the schooling model, and those concepts receive the attention of researchers. There are other concepts on the fringes of the model that fall into the role of schooling but the realm of education writ larger (including the body of work on adult education and learning). These studies are exemplars of the latter and as such they can define a set of structural parameters. That is, what does education look like when one ceases to consider schools? This conversation of context and of education rather than schooling enhances both the discussion of schooling and the ways in which we can work with the concepts of education independently of the institutions that typically claim a monopoly on both the concept and practice of schooling, and in so doing usurp the larger meaning of education.

Nevertheless, using domestic violence shelters as an example of informal learning environments somewhat oversimplifies the transition/translation between formal and informal education. Often, the structural considerations of the two separate worlds seem insurmountable. What informal forms of education seem to have captured is a system (not in the sense of a formal, regimented—sociological—system, but as a loose set of principles) with a differing set of assumptions. These assumptions are in part easily predictable: they assume no taken-for-granted audience; they focus on excitement (or shock) and the unique rather than the mundane or "traditional"; they work intergenerationally, whether by extending the initial activity with materials to be used at home or by crafting the initial activity to work at many levels of understanding (both age and cognitive reasoning); and they focus on capturing the "heart" of an individual. Formal education shares these goals, particularly the last, of capturing hearts (and minds).

Informal learning activities also labor under fewer restrictions (both structural and ideological). First, they take place during comparatively unregulated time, time not "owned" by taxpayers or governed by the state. In this, the activities maintain a relative freedom from structure and interference. Further, the principle of "freedom" must be expanded to encompass the fact that this type of learning occurs not only at the discretion of the learning, but nonlinearly, occurring in spurts of activity or interest.

Second, informal learning experiences capitalize on the need to attract people (since they neither have mandate nor means to compel participation). Instead of viewing this as a liability, the projects that comprise informal education tend to use this principle as a way to explore methods of bringing people in and offering experiences that they might not otherwise have, may enjoy, or are interesting in their uniqueness.

Third, the informal learning activities involve multiage groups. Shelters and projects such as the Clothesline lack the advantage (if it is one) of grouping people by either age or experience. Instead, they welcome all comers, and the activities they provide must engage these other groups. In this, the learning is intergenerational. In the shelters I studied, this single phenomenon—intergenerational learning—formed the pivotal dynamic in the learning process. Shelters had "cohorts" of women, each lending a hand downward to women who are newer than themselves, while receiving a hand up from those "more experienced." This is one way in which the cohort system works; every woman in shelter has participated in the initial mad scramble to put order to their lives. At the same time, women are surrounded by those stretching toward the next goal. In shelters, as chaotic as they are, it seems there is usually someone who has been there longer who knows how to, and will, assist another less experienced women deal with an issue. These residents also serve as models for newer residents, particularly when they are granted special privileges (in one shelter, residents can be placed in "transitional" housing, for example, which is a more independent arm of shelter housing).

Finally, informal activities rely on passion—the truly affective dimension of learning. It has become clear that it is important—if not critical—to capture hearts as well as minds. While projects such as the Clothesline (see chapter 5) do rely on people learning from a single exposure to the shirts hanging on a line, the mission of the group stretches further. If people view the shirts once, leave, and think no more of violence against women, the mission fizzles. Therefore the project attempts to compel both realization and action beyond the timeframe of the single experience. Informal learning is episodic, like life. Projects in the informal education world sometimes rely on single, powerful experiences for learning, while relying on others to continue the learning that they begin.

Translating Formal and Informal Learning

The immediate issue is to uncover any lessons to be learned from shelters where women of varying levels of education, income, and races and ethnicities and coming from many different backgrounds learn together. This challenge to educate across multiple needs and dimensions (yet with severely limited resources) echoes conversations about multiculturalism and urban education (particularly the challenge of poverty). Yet its reach is not limited to these immediate ideas. If there are lessons to be learned from teaching women in shelter, then the structure of shelters challenge many new theories, while shoring up others.

In concrete terms, shelters are small—often fewer than 20 residents, including young children. If shelters, due to their size and resulting intimacy are successful learning environments, how does this reflect on the drawbacks of distance learning?

Shelters operate intergenerationally and across varied needs and learning levels. If shelters, due to this mixed grouping are successful learning environments, questions may be asked about tracking, grouping, and indeed whether, how, or why such distinctions are made.

Domestic violence shelters in particular are most often women-only environments. If shelters, due to their single-sex limitation, are successful learning environments, one may begin to address affirmative action and the question of whether such environments are necessary or good. These are but a few of the links that can be made.

Research is increasingly valuable, and valued, as it is deliberately structured to allow ready application to other environments. To accomplish this, any promising practice—that is, any practice, broadly defined, which is found to be successful—should be grounded in the context where it is successful to allow for replicability or adaptation. This work provides a thorough description of the structural environment of domestic violence shelters to enable this type of translation from one place to another, as well as from one issue to another.

Defining Spaces as Educational

If not as educational spaces, how *do* shelters define themselves? The two shelters I studied intensely both identified themselves primarily as feminist organizations focused on social justice issues—the empowerment of women, fighting back against the social stigma of domestic violence and rape, providing resources for women and the community to interrupt the patriarchal structure, which not only allowed but encouraged the physical, mental, and emotional subjugation of women. Magda Gere Lewis (1992) expresses similar sentiments about her feminist teaching at the university. bell hooks does so as well, and it is easy to name more: Jo Freeman, Pauline Bart, Angela Davis, Michelle Fine, Michéle Foster—both the famous women and the less-well-known women's studies professors who regularly lead students to question existing social structures.

There is no single definition of feminist pedagogy, nor is it necessary to have one. In earlier work, I conclude that feminist teaching is not only contextually situated, but personally unique—that is, perhaps it is teaching *by* feminists. In her recent work examining the practice of another set of feminist teachers, Becky Ropers-Huilman agrees that all degrees of feminist practice fall within the university setting (Ropers-Huilman 1998). It stands to reason, then, that if feminist pedagogy is not limited to a single technique, it is not limited to a single location. Feminist pedagogy, as discussed in the literature, often refers to formal teaching within environments such as the university; indeed, my own earlier work considered this context. However, this work moves beyond formal education into the informal educational environments with the potential for feminist education. Carmen Luke provides ample evidence that pedagogical spaces are not limited to formal educational settings (Luke 1996). She believes, as do I, that learning and teaching are infused throughout daily living:

> Learning and teaching, in my estimation, are the very intersubjective core relations of everyday life. They exist beyond the classroom, are always gendered and intercultural. (1996, p. 7)

In the particular case of domestic violence, another of her insights is valuable:

> And it is this struggle for place, identity, and, indeed, survival—this learning to make the self in relation to the overlapping, sometimes congruent and often contradictory discourses that variously combine to constrain and enable subject positions and identities—that is the very substance of everyday life for most people in what are now called postmodern conditions. (1996, pp. 10–11)

The question I wrestle with in this work is how such learning struggles take place in shelters. At all stages of residence, women leave shelter. A clear pattern emerges: there is relatively high turnover in the first two weeks of a woman's stay. Women who make it through this time can be expected to move forward with plans for a different life, although this growth has setbacks; women have personality conflicts with each other, staff, and resident cliques. Some residents then enter transitional housing, while others leave the shelter and reenter the community. Some leave to join family or friends. Some rejoin their abusers. Some move on to different forms of shelter. All seem to learn while they pause for a brief interlude in shelter.

Literature on feminist pedagogy provides a number of referent points, defining what is and could be considered feminist teaching. Some of these referent points define what occurred in these shelters. However, I inadvertently approached this study inductively—without an explicit framework. This text is based on nearly seven years of work in and concerning domestic violence shelters. I did not enter the world of abuse as a researcher; I entered as a volunteer, a concerned woman, and an outraged feminist. Yet, my researcher's mind accompanied me into shelter, where I sat with woman after woman, cohort after cohort, and realized I had found myself in a learning environment. After that realization, I began to formalize my work, which encompasses two shelters where I worked, and numerous conversations with others about shelters they had experienced.

I believe I was fortunate to have stumbled into this research because I left myself open to the kinds of actions that might constitute feminist teaching within these shelter environments. Thus, I ended up with a somewhat different set of characteristics of feminist teaching than have been found in the literature, although there is clear overlap. Since the majority of the literature examines feminist teaching within formal education, it is useful to quickly review some of the major markers of what has traditionally been considered feminist teaching. The research here does not exhaust the limits of feminist teaching. In discussing informal education[1] it is critical to note that this discussion of practice is not about how various feminist projects "measure up" to the theory on feminist pedagogy. However, the literature does serve as a backdrop to consider feminist education.

A continuum of feminist ideas about education encompasses those under the more moderate rubric of "equitable education," "gender-balanced education," or such terms as well as the most radical liberatory education (the basis for much work with women in developing countries). Yet the definitions used within this continuum are in constant motion and have radically shifted in the past five years. One indicator of this shift is in the most moderate, equity-based writings, which have moved from a deficit model of girlhood ("girls are falling behind") to a more proactive stance ("the point is not to compare girls' weaknesses to boys' strengths") (AAUW researched by Sattler 1998). What has generally remained constant are the parameters of the theory behind feminist pedagogy(ies); as Kenway and Modra write, activism is at the heart of feminist education:

> Feminists believe that women are located unequally in the social formation, often devalued, exploited and oppressed. Education systems, the knowledge which they offer and the practices which constitute them, are seen to be complicit in this. . . . Feminism, then, is a social theory and a social movement, but it is also a personal political practice. For feminist educators, feminism is a primary lens through which the world is interpreted and acted upon. (1992, p. 139)

---

1. Informal education, for the purposes of this paper, is defined as learning and teaching that take place intentionally (in semistructured settings) outside of the realm of "formal education." The audience for informal education is quite different in terms of assessment, demand, and needs.

This statement recognizes the value feminist theorists place on education as a route to social change. As Maher and Tetreault describe it, feminist pedagogy is woman-centered pedagogy:

> What has made feminist pedagogy unique ... has been its attention to the particular needs of women students and its grounding in feminist theory as the basis for its multidimensional and positional view of the construction of classroom knowledge. (1994, p. 9)

What, though, is (are) the(se) route(s)? What are the particular needs of women students? Again along the continuum, key indicators of feminist pedagogy seem to be based both on feminist content and process dimensions. Content is arguably the simplest dimension, including such topics as explicitly political issues of power, representation, and the female body. By this criteria, any pedagogical setting in which the content is the politics and prevention of domestic violence is feminist. Process dimensions (what is typically called pedagogy) center on tactics such as inclusion (e.g., representation in the curriculum and in class discussions); intimacy (e.g., use of small groups); voice (the sharing of stories and the use of authentic experiences in a pedagogical setting); authority/critiques of power (both of institutions and of classroom relationships, often resulting in different role expectations for both teachers and students); positionality (the recognition that we all speak and understand from multiple locations of gender, race, class, sexuality, and experiences); and mastery (the idea that material is to be explored rather than mastered, and that expertise is multidimensional) (Maher and Tretrault 1994; Kenway and Modra 1992; Gore 1992; Middleton 1993; Weiler 1989; Culley 1985, Shrewsbury 1987; Schniedewind 1987; Grumet 1988; Maher 1985, 1987; Ropers-Huilman, 1998; Sattler 1996).

These theories, however, arise from a particular location at particular times and types of institutions. They have primarily been developed by university-based women's studies professors (until recently white women), responsible for teaching relatively young students. The university system itself is relevant: the literature with which I am familiar is shaped by formal structures such as semesters or quarters, "courses," "syllabi," and other artifacts (e.g., articles on how to teach a course on antisexism). None, for example, are written from the perspective of more open campuses (e.g., those with Great Books curricula or loosely defined liberal arts exploration) with the exception of bell hooks's work during her time at Oberlin. None in my awareness arises from historically black colleges or universities; although Maher and Tretrault do analyze feminist teaching at Spelman College, a historically black institution with the addition of being single-sex, the analysis is external rather than internal. Students of such faculty, historically also primarily female and white, also are privileged in the sense that they have access to higher education.

Theory, Madeline Grumet writes compellingly, is location-specific:

> Theory is cultivated in the public world. Theory grows where it is planted, soaking up the nutrients in the local soil, turning to the local light. A theory of education that is cultivated in the academy, the library, or the laboratory accommodates to its environment. (1988, p. 14)

The politics of location are critical, as Audre Lorde (1981), Magda Gere Lewis (1993), and others have argued convincingly. Kathleen Weiler writes that "feminist pedagogy as it has developed in the United States provides a historically situated example of a critical pedagogy in practice" (1991/1998, p. 118). Consider the example of Marilyn Schuster and Susan Van Dyne's early "stages of curriculum transformation," since adapted by Rosser and others, which is clearly shaped within a university context: (1) absence of women not noted; (2) search for missing women; (3) women as disadvantaged, subordinate group; (4) women studied on own terms; (5) women as challenge to disciplines; and (6) transformed, "balanced" curriculum (1984/1998, p. 85). They conclude with a definition of a transformed course as follows.

A transformed course would:

- be self-conscious about *methodology;*
- present changed content in a *changed context;*
- develop an *interdisciplinary perspective;*
- pay meaningful attention to intersections of *race, class, and cultural differences within gender;*
- study new subjects in their *own terms;*
- *test paradigms* rather that merely 'add on' women figures or issues . . . ;
- make the student's experience and learning process part of the explicit content of the course. (1984/1998, p. 94, emphases in original)

Even beyond the category of "curriculum," or "course," the types of action called for are most useful within the postsecondary context and less so within feminist shelters, which have their own pedagogical process.

More similar to shelters, but still distant, is Eva Young and Mariwilda Padilla's analysis of *Mujeres Unidas en Acción* (Women United in Action), a group of Latinas in Massachusetts organized to provide educational services to low-income Latinas. They state that their (feminist) participatory approach is an interactive one:

> Women are given the opportunity and are encouraged to express their opinions and ideas at all levels of the agency. For example, classroom curriculum is developed around students' needs as articulated by them. For women who have never before been asked to express an opinion, doing so and being respected for it makes them active participants and is empowering. Providing learning experiences that promote critical thinking skills allows women to make decisions about their own lives and take a more active and assertive role in them. (1990/1998, p. 99)

Mujeres Unidas en Acción moves beyond the literal content of their courses—English as a Second Language (ESL) and General Equivilency Diploma (GED) preparation—in a way that extends feminist pedagogy located at universities.

> Specifically, many women who come to Mujeres want only to learn English; they do not want to deal with other issues and problems at home. Their participation in class discussions allows them to realize that the problems each of them may face at home or in their lives are not theirs alone . . . [and] that the solutions can only be found collectively. (1990/1998, p. 105)

These disparate examples begin to illustrate the differences that environmental structures make; *Mujeres*, for example, has no curriculum and its courses are only loosely structured. Some shelters are positioned even further along the organizational continuum in terms of their amount of structure. One important element of structural comparison is in who does the teaching and who the audience is. In *Mujeres*, for example, teachers were Latinas, resulting in a somewhat equal teaching relationship. In this Latinas-teaching-Latinas, women-teaching-women relationship, it becomes possible to begin on common ground.

Shelter workers, like residents in most abuse-oriented shelters, are women; many also are formerly battered women. Like the women in *Mujeres*, they can begin on common ground. These women are the conductors on the feminist railroad; their work includes listening as well as speaking, understanding as well as advocating. In their narratives, shelter workers describe their experiences with battered women, including their personal journeys into knowledge of being battered and their own survival as well as the ways in which they teach women to help themselves.

Formal Training

Where life stories vary, training can be a unifying and invariant piece of shelter workers' lives. It is important to recognize that even in shelters where "lay" staff predominate, staff stand at the junction of life experience and formal training. In particular, for staff whose basic experience with domestic violence stems from personal experience, formal training is important for a number of reasons, including so that the staffer can separate out her solution in specific from the solutions that other women may choose. In many instances, staff receive the same training that volunteers receive. (Appendix A of this book reviews the basis for much of this training, which would also include specifics on the shelter, the need for confidentiality, and other information.) While this chapter will not spend much time examining the training or professional development of shelter workers, there is one component of one training in which I conducted participant observation that struck a chord at the time and which resonates throughout this book. The group leader drew a large triangle on a flip chart. At each point, beginning with the top, she wrote one of these words: victim, abuser, savior.

Exhibit: The problematic relationship between resident and shelter worker.

These, she told us, were the only three roles that women in shelter, particularly at the beginning, recognized as legitimate. Shelter work, she told us, was about staying outside the triangle and not accepting these roles. The tension is particularly between savior and abuser. Shelter workers lean toward trying to be saviors, saving women from violence, abuse, and their own lives. Women, however, cannot be saved; they only can save themselves. This is the meaning of transformation. As Emma Goldman wrote, "Liberty will not descend to a people, a people must raise themselves to liberty."

There But For the Grace of God

Shelter workers, whether they have been personally abused or not (and many have), depend on their experiences with "generations" of shelter residents, which gives them a deep and penetrating understanding of the cycle of violence, and a pragmatic view of the ways to escape. Their experiences, in turn, make them excellent teachers. Shelter workers who are formerly battered women themselves bring their experiences to work with them. At the same time, formerly battered women are a powerful icon of success; they are strong women, having escaped and "made it." Their stories have breadth, and depth, and most importantly the weight of experience. For some residents, this experience is the single most important characteristic shelter workers have, and the singular reason that residents open up to the staff.

Women who have themselves been abused and who work in shelters must choose whether to tell their stories or not. For some, these stories become more painful in the retelling, while for others, the opposite is true. For still others, their own stories are eventually replaced by the fresher stories of other women. In the following narrative, a formerly battered women relates how she uses her story as a teaching tool for residents:

> *Staff (formerly battered woman): I tell people each part of my life you know I, I learn by it and I don't mind sharing it with someone if this is also going to help them and they can see that they are not by themself on things also. Because a lot of times women, women want to know that they are not by themself and that whatever they have gone through that they thought was shameful was that somebody else has gone through it or even worse because then they're not as ashamed and so and, and that's just the whole thing and I guess that's the reason why I talk with them and share (laughing) everything.*

The presence of formerly battered women on staff reinforces the important idea—key to residents—that this is not a problem of *one* woman and *one* man, but is a larger social problem. Staff use their stories in two ways: to shore up their own strength in helping women to help themselves; and to show women what survival is.

> *Staff: I can actually sit down and identify with somebody saying, "He beat me in my face until I couldn't feel it anymore. He choked me unconscious. He spit on me. He busted my lip open." I mean, I can feel their pain.*

> *Staff: Talking with women at the shelter and specially ones that have children, you know because everyone has come in with children I can relate things to them you know and I see it because I see it in my daughter you know and so when I talk with them and I tell them you know. And I, I mean things that I've done, things I've done in the past, I talk with them the same way, I talk with the women about anything and everything you know that I've gone through. Even from a*

> *child on up you know and I'm gonna tell you something that people found out later that shocked me and how I am so sane.*

For other staffers, their own life stories are secondary to those of the women:

> *Staff (formerly battered woman): I don't even share my story, you know, with the ladies. I just, I understand what they're going through with the battering, but to say, you know, "well, I'm here because—" well, I came here because I was a battered woman and that was part of what it was, but it was mostly, you know, being able to help the women. But I don't think I actually bring that now. I think it's done. It's far from my mind because I've heard so many stories, mine is gone.*

These life experiences are important in the shelter context. First, is the felt need, both by residents and workers, to be "real." For residents, this need is most often expressed as a desire to work with (and sometimes only with) those workers who have "been there" and thus understand. Staff credibility is of tantamount importance to shelter residents. Residents emphasized two forms: trusting shelter workers because of the workers' own experiences with violence; and trusting staff with the details of their lives. The first issue is a key strength of shelters with many formerly battered women on staff. As such, these staff members have incredibly high, positive credibility among the women in shelter, many of whom have few people they can trust. Hence, someone who has "been there" and understands their internal conflicts and confusing circumstances is a welcome addition to their lives. A returning resident puts it succinctly:

> *Res: I don't want to see a psychiatrist or therapist unless the therapist has been through some of what I've been through. But, with the women here, most of them have been through what we've been through, so they can come and relate. 'Cause I don't want to talk to a person—I don't want a person giving me advice or information that hasn't been through some of what I've been through because you don't know what I'm going through. She don't know what I'm feeling, she don't know what I've felt. So, it feels good that I can come back and still talk to the same women that when I left here was here.*

The importance of credibility also extends to other workers and volunteers across shelter programs. For example, many women expressed their skepticism when parenting groups were run by a woman with no children.

Residents felt that the instructor knew the theory but could not understand what it was like to become frustrated with one's child—primarily because she could go home and leave the children, while they could not:

> Res.:   *I did not like [parenting group].*
> Int.:   *Why?*
> Res.:   *Well, [the leader] didn't have any kids, she's very nice but I just don't figure you going to tell me what to do when you don't have any kids; just because you work with them you don't have to go home with them.*

Many women simply do not want assistance from those who (they feel) do not understand their situation. Further, women who have "been there" often have valuable advice to give about how to accomplish particular tasks. (In one case, where several "professionals" failed to help a shelter resident obtain important documents, a staffer who was a formerly battered woman was almost immediately successful in procuring the necessary paperwork.) For staff, the philosophy is to empower residents so that they understand, and can use, the system that exists outside the shelter doors. This sense of being "streetwise" is conveyed through the following passage:

> Staff: *I am somewhat on their level, you know. And me talking more streetwise for them. They understand more street than someone that comes in and try to do this whole dialogue or diagram for them and they're like, what are you talking about, you know. And you get them, you tell them this, you know, this is the real deal. This is the real deal, you know.*

This life experience, then, is critical to the shelter as a teaching and learning organization. In this way, learning is extremely pragmatic—if you have "been there," you may show others how to make it through. (At the same time, this assumption is somewhat dangerous. Consider the case in formal education where a white teacher brings in African-American topics and literature and is told that she cannot possibly understand and therefore cannot teach. While it is true that experience-based understanding is very different from a more peripheral perspective, one cannot only teach what one knows from direct experience. This argument is beyond the scope of this work, although its implications are critical for teaching and learning across environments.) The telling of such stories—whether of residents or staff—is pivotal to the teaching and learning that goes on in shelters. Life experiences, the pieces of lives, are both curriculum and materials in the world of domestic violence education.

Shelter Work as a Teaching Profession

Shelter staff are not credentialed with teaching certificates, nor have they in most cases studied pedagogy. However, their teaching is deliberate. In the two shelters represented in this work, training requirements differ markedly. In the first, the majority of shelter workers are new "MSWs," or women with their master's degrees in social work. In general they are trained as counselors, often working on their counseling licensure and using their shelter work to fulfil requirements necessary for certification. In the second, the majority of shelter workers are formerly battered women with little formal training other than that offered to volunteers. As might be imagined, these women go about their jobs somewhat differently—but not as differently as the preceding outline of their basic credentials might suggest. There is a distinct symmetry across shelters, expressed by the women in this study and by other shelter workers I have spoken with over the years. The profession pivots around women. Women are clients and workers, teachers and learners, formerly battered women and those currently being abused. Women surround each other in the shelter environment, helped by policies ensuring women-only environments in many shelters, which may (as these two shelters do) exclude even adolescent male children for safety and comfort reasons. This women-oriented environment is a critical component of the highly political forms of teaching and learning that take place in shelters, as described in this chapter.

Shelter workers identify themselves as counselors (whether formal or lay), social workers, or advocates; they identify themselves as other-than-teacher. However, on closer examination, the two professions share a great deal. The social work profession links to the teaching profession by its low status (predominance of women, a focus on helping others, and a relatively low wage) but, more interestingly, in terms of actual tasks. In this work, I spoke and worked with women who do not, by and large, identify as teachers—yet the work that I watched them do is centered in teaching and learning.[2] Rereading the transcripts of the interviews with residents, I am struck anew at the ground that must be covered in each interview—ground that is covered by these shelter workers as they piece together stories, and then lives, teaching as they go. At this point, I draw the distinction between varying "types" of shelter workers to mark a simple yet critical factor: despite their different starting points, the commonality of women-helping-women

---

2. I do not hesitate to add that teachers perform many of the duties of social workers, as well, particularly as the role of schools expands to ensuring the health and welfare of its students.

results in a strikingly similar pedagogy. bell hooks reminds us that Thich Nhat Hanh referred to teachers as healers, and quotes Paolo Friere:

> Authentic help means that all who are involved help each other mutually, growing together into the common effort to understand the reality which they seek to transform. Only through such praxis—in which those who help and those who are being helped help each other simultaneously—can the act of helping become free from the distortion in which the helper dominates the helped. (1994, p. 54)

Such is the case in these shelters.

CHAPTER 5

Sharing Secrets and Making Noise

I woke up this morning with my mind stayed on freedom
Hallelu! Hallelu! Hallelu!
                                —African-American spiritual

Women do not always speak aloud in telling their stories. Voices
require neither sound nor words. Chapter 2 mentioned women's use
of household objects as forms of expression. Slaves did so as well (see chapter 7). A readily identifiable source of women's voices can be found in
quilts.

In years past, the best quilts were cared for as precious objects, stored
away in chests and drawers, away from sunlight. They were brought out for
special guests, or they formed part of a bride's trousseau. Today, quilts are
used more decoratively, hanging on walls in offices, museums, and homes.
The stories they tell extend beyond female spaces, instead displayed for
public view. Faith Ringgold, whose story quilts are known for their combination of intimacy and political prose, undertakes artistic satire simultaneously with political statements in her French Collection. Her quilt, *The
Picnic at Giverny (The French Collection, Part I: #3)*, satirizes Manet's *Le
Dejeuner Sur L'Herbe*, which portrays two fully clothed men picnicking
with two nude women, all of whom were well-known. Ringgold reverses
the politics of the piece by painting clothed, lifelike women from her own
life in the center of this quilt, with the nude figure of Picasso. On the quilt,
she inscribes the following pointed text:

[The women] are speaking of *la liberation et la liberte* for women.
Sometime we think we are free, until we spread our wings and are
cut down in mid air. . . . Should I paint some of the great and tragic
issues of our world? A black man toting a heavy load that has
pinned him to the ground? Or a black woman nursing the world's
population of children? Or the two of them together as slaves,
building a beautiful world for others to live free? *Non*! I want to

paint something that will inspire—liberate! I want to do some of this WOMEN ART. *Magnifique!*

Ringgold's work is an example of women's stories not only as individual consciousness-raising, but as a learning tool available to larger audiences who also must choose to participate. Generally hung in museums but also installed in public spaces such as New York City's subway system, such work may evoke any reaction imaginable. Such work is part of a large body of political messaging, including museum exhibits, sidewalk theater, performance art, and the like. These activities or visual displays—leaving aside the deliberately interactive—are themselves static, existing apart from the response of the audience. What is lost is the intimacy of two-way communication. What is gained is the potential to reach those who would not ordinarily seek particular learning experiences.

As outreach, Ringgold thrusts the stories of women and African Americans into a public forum, where the stories demand a hearing. If domestic violence is to end, women's stories of violence must not be limited to the space within shelter walls. In moving beyond the shelter community, women's stories can and do become educational tools for a broader audience.

This kind of informal learning, although it is the core of art education has not received much attention either in the U.S. educational research community or in the larger discussion about education. Britain has led the research done to date, while work has begun in the United States as well (cf. Crane et al., 1994; Falk and Dierking, 1993a, 1993b; Gennaro, 1982; Jacobson, 1990). This learning community remains largely unexamined, partially because its results are not measured nor measurable in terms of direct student outcomes. Its effects are diffuse but nonetheless critical to understanding the broader picture of education and life-long learning. Informal education does not have a captive audience; nor does it receive the level of bureaucratic scrutiny of the classroom. As such, it has had the advantage of developing in an atmosphere of relative freedom. Some of this research points out factors that influence the extent to which people engage in, and benefit from, such informal activities. Not surprisingly, these factors include the set of experiences about what they did, how they felt, and what they thought—and what they do with the resulting information (Crane et al., 1994; Crane, Nicholson, Chen, and Bitgood, 1994; Falk and Dierking, 1993a, 1993b; Zantal-Wiener, Sattler, and Yin, 1996).

Political projects have successfully borrowed these techniques of women creating objects that both tell a story and create community, and of inviting public readings of these objects with the goal of eliciting a reaction. Perhaps the most outstanding example of such a project in the field of domestic violence is the Clothesline Project, now a worldwide community of women telling their experiences of violence using a common artistic medium, putting names and faces on statistics of domestic and other forms of violence.

The Clothesline Project

The Clothesline Project is one in a series of community-based efforts to raise awareness of women's issues, including domestic violence. In its work, it draws on a long line of informal learning environments and reinforces the idea that learning, and listening, come in many forms.

The Clothesline Project consists of a collection of shirts made by women who have suffered violence. Some shirts additionally are made by the friends of women who have suffered violence, particularly women who have died. The shirts hang on clotheslines, attached with clothespins, as old-fashioned laundry still done in backyards around the country. The shirts "air" the women's "dirty laundry," speaking of violence, its effects and, most times, their survival. The mission of the Clothesline Project is to engage people in the stories of women's violence and survival, and to create awareness of both the problem and the desire and ability to act toward a variety of solutions.

It is not odd, given the history of women's domestic space and the crafts fashioned within these spaces (see chapter 2), that one way to reclaim voice for women who name themselves victims—and survivors—of violence is the Clothesline Project, an exemplar of such a craft. By refusing to accept traditional definitions of women's work as second-class, women set their own terms for the debate. For example, quilting, sewing, weaving, and other "traditional" women's acts have been long disparaged as utilitarian, and as craft, not art (cf. Chicago 1980, 1996). Many devalue women's work automatically, *because* it is done by women. Women who demand recognition and an audience defy this categorization. As a form of women's material storytelling, the clothesline takes its place in a long line of symbolic domestic creations, indicating that the so-called "separate sphere" of domestic life harbors a power of its own.

The origin of the group that calls itself the Clothesline Project is an important framework for the way shirts are created, displayed, and their significance. A group in Cape Cod, Massachusetts, initiated the project in 1990 to communicate the "horrific extent of violence perpetrated against women" (Clothesline Project 1995), sparked by this statistic:

> 51,000 women were murdered in the United States by their husbands or lovers during the 16 years of the Vietnam War. The War

itself took 58,000 Americans. (Maryland Men's Anti-Rape Resource Center 1995)

Leaving aside the controversy of the Vietnam War, these women questioned why history records wars, memorials commemorate men killed during wars, and veterans receive special privileges for their service—while nearly the same number of women were dying unrecognized, unmemorialized, and in silence. They determined that women should receive their own memorial, one that symbolized the nature of the violence they suffered, and that would at the same time educate others about the horrors of an ongoing war here at home.

On October 8 of that year, the Cape Cod group hung a clothesline filled with 30 shirts describing the violence encountered by women in their community. These shirts, blowing in the northeast wind, were the first in a series of "dirty laundry" women were increasingly willing to share with their neighbors, families, communities, and friends. The concept quickly became global, displayed in 1992 to the International Congress of the Women's International League for Peace and Freedom (WILPF), in Geneva at the United Nations (UN) Human Rights Conference in 1993, and in Beijing as part of the UN's International Conference on Women. There are ever expanding clothesline projects in countries outside the United States as well, including Canada, Costa Rica, Cuba, England, Israel, the Philippines, and Tanzania.

This project, similar in nature to the AIDS quilt, has expanded through a number of local organizations, including domestic violence shelters, and is run in a grassroots manner. Fundamentally, their activity centers on creating the space and freedom in which victim/survivors (and their friends and family) can create t-shirts that tell their stories. These shirts are then hung on clotheslines, symbolizing at once women's work, women's stories and their fight against violence, and the airing of "dirty laundry." Six thousand of an estimated 30,000 shirts were displayed in the 1995 National Organization for Women's Rally Against Violence Against Women. The response of the onlookers, ranging from rage to tears, testified to the power of women's narratives, the struggle for survival, and the effects of community education. The shirts are color-coded: white for women who have died violently; red, orange, or pink for women raped or sexually assaulted; blue or green for survivors of incest or child sexual abuse; yellow or beige to represent battering or assault; and purple or lavender for lesbian bashing/hate crimes. As of February 1, 1995, it was estimated that there were 246 lines in 46 states; 35,150 total shirts. At that time, the line stretched for 13.25 miles. If there were a shirt for every woman raped, battered, or murdered during 1992 (the latest year for which FBI statistics are available) it is estimated that the clothesline would stretch for 1,774 miles—from Washington, D.C., to Denver, Colorado. These shirts are educative in two forms: to the women who create them and to the people who see them.

The education earned by the women who make the shirts is clear. They cry, scream, and sing. I have watched women create poetry—and I have watched them take the scissors and cut gaping holes in shirts. I have helped women hang their still-wet shirts on the line and have cried with them. As one viewer phrased it,

> *You can see the women are in stages of their grief. It is like a wall of silence surrounding the shirts. Their grief is so powerful. The most powerful thing is that these are women like me, from all walks of life. They're not people on Oprah. You could see it on the crowd's faces; they knew something was going on.*

An Education in Silence[1]

The first national display of the Clothesline Project took place in conjunction with a typical Washington, D.C., scene: an enthusiastic, noisy, adrenaline-fueled group of activists rallying on the Mall. While the rally went on around the space, within it was eerily quiet and quietly powerful. Media described this same dynamic (*Cape Cod Chronicle* 1994; *Cape Cod Times* 1994; *Dennis Register* 1995; *Harwich Oracle* 1994; *NOW Times*, 1995). Visual and verbal reactions to the shirts differed radically from the rest of the rally, drawing casual onlookers into deeper involvement. One such onlooker described the line's visual power:

> *Two things. The white shirts. The color coding, white for women who have died. And the process . . . I told them I'd work two hours. I worked three days and now I'm a project volunteer . . . I couldn't sleep Saturday night (after viewing all the shirts).*
>
> *Held at gunpoint for four hours, brutalized, violated, raped, forever changed.*

These women's stories were speaking louder than the crowd. There was a hush around the Clothesline display, in the middle of a loud rally against violence against women. The shirts were in some ways as graphic as war

---

1. The data in this section was collected during the Clothesline Project's first national display, during the N.O.W. rally against violence against women in 1995, and through my subsequent work with the D.C. Clothesline Project until April 1997 (at that time the D.C. project merged with a newer line in Arlington, Virginia). During the rally, I worked as a "marshall," assigned to the Clothesline Project as a counselor.

photographs, and the silence was as thick as one might find near the Vietnam Veterans' Memorial burdened with its stories. The stories are powerful, so much so that the women become individuals to viewers.

I made this shirt so no one can tell me to be quiet anymore.

The goal of this education is social change, but also to serve as a catalyst for reflection and action. These shirts have two messages; they teach in two ways. Explicitly the message is simple: there is a cycle of violence, it's everywhere in society, and it's not okay to be hit. Women die and must be remembered. The implicit message is equally (if not more) powerful: it's okay to fight back. Women can and do survive.

The only time I bought new glasses was when you punched me in the face.

Stories with Faces and Names

In this project, shirt-making itself is a highly intimate act between a woman and her internal sense of privacy, balanced with wanting or needing to tell her story. Many women, after making their shirts, keep them for some time before releasing them for display. Some of these women have told me that they needed to be sure that they were ready not only to tell their story, but to tell it to others in such a public venue.

Most shirt-making takes place in private venues, including domestic violence shelters. The women at one shelter, for example, participate in shirt-making as part of their support group, and another way of consciousness-raising. Others do so in rape support groups, counseling or therapy groups, or other organized groups who use the shirt-making as therapeutic outlets. In some communities, the Clothesline Project acts in coalition with shelters for battered women, holding shirt-making sessions so that the women have access to these external means of telling their stories. Speaking aloud entails risk for the women in shelter; their stories are often fresh and new, barely scabbed over and ready to bleed again at the slightest scratch. Yet many women report that the creation of their shirts is freeing, as a declaration of survival. I watched one woman, who selected a white shirt, spell out her sister's name in a cross-shaped acrostic. She had survived; her sister had not.

In spite of these multiple opportunities, freedom does not arrive on a set schedule. Doubts and fears linger. Some women tell their stories in order to regain freedom, while some must feel freer in order to speak at all. Therefore, women often don't tell their stories immediately, nor is there a predictable sequence of events leading up to their revelations. These multiple patterns come forth in the Project as well. Although many women plan their stories carefully, such plans often give way to a torrent of emotion and the immediacy of needing to tell one's story. Lisa, a leader in the D.C. Clothesline Project, was one such woman who painstakingly planned her shirt. It would have an appliqué of a flower, be made of a certain fabric, and of a particular design. She had chosen and purchased fabric and other materials, waiting, she said, for the right time. The shirt in her mind never materialized, although her planning and details were a meticulous process she hid behind. One day she literally left her space as a Clothesline Project volunteer, chose a shirt, and poured out her story in paint. Lisa's shirt hangs on the line. Every time she uses it to tell her story, she shakes; but in the making of the shirt, and its statement, Lisa demonstrated to herself, and the world, that she had started to heal. She had survived. Like the stories of women in shelter, once the dam is breached, the stories come pouring out, virtually unstoppable. In this rush to storytelling and revelation, learning becomes translated from private to public, and its power is felt in both spheres. The messages on shirts are often simple, handwritten by women in marker and paint or fashioned from children's clothing (often for incest). One shirt is, quite graphically, the bloodstained shirt worn by a woman at the time she was killed. It was hung by her friends, in her memory. Some of the shirts are blank; others cover every surface with words, pictures, memories.

Teach me to cry and when I have learned to cry, teach me to dance, so that I may dance in the puddle of my tears.

The project itself writes that women's voice and expression is of direct, and paramount, concern:

Few avenues exist for women to speak openly and honestly about the violence they have experienced. Making a shirt and hanging it on a publicly displayed clothesline becomes an integral part of a woman's healing. It is a complex process, from the initial decision to make a shirt, through the design and creation of the shirt; even letting go of the finished shirt and turning it over to their local Clothesline Project is a wrenching experience for many shirtmakers. Finally seeing their story hanging in unison with the stories of other local women, viewed by family, neighbors, and strangers alike, allows many survivors to own their own pain and to express their anger in hopes that someday no woman will have to bear the agony of violence.

Convicted for stealing $19.00, two cameras and a jacket, but not for rape.

The shirts symbolize both process and lesson: women healing and women telling their stories. En masse, the women—and the shirts—are a reminder of the many, often unheard voices of the millions they represent.

Transcending Words

As powerful as the messages themselves are, the shirt-as-medium itself cannot be overemphasized. The shirt itself, as a symbol of ordinary life as well as women's work and dirty laundry, carries part of the message. Quilts similarly symbolize and carry part of women's everyday teaching to other women. Messages play on both the visual and intellectual levels. As a teaching element, the visual is often undersold, despite rhetoric about (and attempts at) multimodal teaching and learning. Visual representation is a critical element identified in gender equity within education. Sadker and Sadker (1994) noted six areas of common current forms of bias in curriculum materials that also can be extended to classroom and school settings, as well as other educational contexts more generally. The six areas are:

- *Invisibility*—omitting women and minority groups in textual materials, discussion topics, and displays;
- *Stereotyping*—assigning traditional and rigid roles or attributes to groups;
- *Imbalance/Selectivity*—presenting only one interpretation of an issue, situation, or group of people;
- *Unreality*—an unrealistic portrayal of our history and our contemporary life experience;
- *Fragmentation/Isolation*—separating discussions and issues related to minorities and women from the main body of the discussion and/or text; and
- *Linguistic Bias*—using only or predominately masculine terms and pronouns, which in essence deny the participation of women in society.

These factors influence students' and teachers' abilities to learn and to teach, and present barriers to equity. In external settings, such as the Clothesline Project, nearly all of these factors are addressed. However, the visual imagery presented by the shirts, together with their texts and embedded images, is particularly poignant. In working with multiply- and differently-literate women, it becomes clear that women's stories, told in this graphic way, reach across many, sometimes unseen, boundaries.

The 1995 national display in Washington, D.C., included shirts from a number of countries. Many of those in the crowd, myself included, could not read many of the shirts—those in Hebrew, Spanish, and many other languages. Yet the shirts spoke. Even without words, the stories echoed across continents and borders, state and county lines. When a woman asked if I could read Hebrew, and offered to translate the shirts for me, the words of women I knew and those on the other shirts were repeated. One shirt that compelled me had no words at all; it was a red shirt with a heart cut out of both sides. The viewer could see the shirt, and through the cut-out heart the rest of the clothesline and the absence of life, and love, and hope. The clothesline droops under the pedagogy of shared stories, even in silence. Like a quilt, it stretches across different women as a reminder of commonality, as well as a wake-up call to listen, and act.

Teaching with T-Shirts

Cloth shirts are not the only ones crafted in such settings. In at least one case, the Clothesline Project also has been used in the most formal of educational settings: classrooms. One college instructor had her students make paper "shirts" for fictional characters:

> A group of students in my introductory literature class are preparing a presentation on the Clothesline Project in which they are going to ask their classmates to join them in making paper t-shirts for women and children in fiction who have been the victims of sexual, physical, mental abuse. They are going to begin the class by naming women whose stories they are reading for this project (Pecola in Toni Morrison's *The Bluest Eye*, Bone in Dorothy Allison's *Bastard out of Carolina*, etc.) and then invite their classmates to add other names—shirts to their paper clothesline.

This classroom eventually did use the Clothesline Project model of presenting stories of violence through the creation and display of storied shirts:

> Four students in my English Literature class presented a workshop on the Clothesline Project this semester and as a class we made a paper clothesline project—a powerful experience. One of the students in the group is a survivor of abuse—her first paper was about going to court to have a restraining order placed against her "boyfriend." The class response was powerful. I still have the paper t-shirts hanging in my office. In fact since then other students have come in to add more shirts. The project was interesting in lots of ways—one of the students made a shirt for a young boy in a novel that he had just finished reading—so part of the conversation in class focused on whether or not people believed that the clothesline project ought to be "genderless."

In this setting, the formal and informal educational worlds met successfully, proving in this instance that translation from the informal world is both possible and useful. Informal education is constructed in a way that includes simple acts, which often are forgotten or overlooked in the structures that weigh down formal educational environments—K–12 and postsecondary education alike.

I spoke with these students to gauge their reactions to learning and other issues. Through e-mail conversations, these students responded to their classroom-based experiences with the Clothesline Project. Their responses were directed at describing their own experiences and analyzing whether or not they considered their participation in the Clothesline Project to be educational. One sophomore from New Hampshire studying environmental conservation wrote the following:

> The clothesline project in our English class started out as a group presentation on our collective topic of relationships. My individual project was on female friendships in literature, as I started I read many stories such as *Fried Green Tomatoes* by Fannie Flagg and a short story by Maria Bruno called "The Feeder" both that had women helping friends out [of] abusive relationships [and] I realized that this is a subject that I would like to study more. As we talked with in our group we found that other people in the group were dealing with stories with violence against women including *The Yellow Wall Paper* by Gilman and the novel *Joy Luck Club*. At this point our presentation date was coming up fast and [the instructor] suggested that we model the project after the real clothesline project. Our goal at this point was to show a relationship between men and women that is often hidden but is very common in today's society.

> I can only tell you what I learned from talking about the stories, giving the presentation and writing a journal about some of the women who got a paper t-shirt, myself coming to college trapped by an abusive boyfriend and how talking and reading about things that relate to my own experiences has helped in my healing process (which I believe it has). As I started my journal it was about, as I said above, female friendships in literature, but as I read about these women it became more about myself, and focused on a subject that I had not really talked about for a year but was always there in the back of my head, how it felt to be isolated from friends and how easier escape becomes when you know some one is there to help you, which is what I found here at college. I realized after the project how much my hall director, who had been there, meant

to me. So you can see that the clothesline project presentation to the class was only a part of the knowledge I gained in reading the stories.

[Do you consider yourself a teacher?]

I think everyone can be a teacher, by taking their own experiences and helping others understand feelings they might not know how to deal with. But I hope that our project helped the women in our class see there is help for domestic violence and that it helped the men see the pain that is suffered because of their actions.

This student's comments reinforce those of the women in shelter, in the pragmatics of abuse—needing external help and support—as well as the inward/outward nature of education. Her concern that she teach and be taught, and that learning be shared, albeit in different ways, by those in the class reminds us that feminist education in these settings occurs in relationship, and that this dimension is fundamental. From her story and those of the other students, it appears that the Clothesline Project is a powerful device within formal as well as informal settings.

Thinking Outside the Box

Why look at other environments for insight on public schools? The current reform efforts within schooling and educational systems are well-documented. In fact, the Goals 2000 toolkit identifies 26 "major milestones in national educational reform" between 1983 and 1990, and another 15 between 1991 and 1993 (Goals 2000, 1993). These reform milestones encompass reform efforts familiar to those conversant with education over the past 15 years: "A Nation at Risk"; the Coalition of Essential Schools; "A Nation Prepared"; the National Council of Teachers of Mathematics (NCTM) standards; expansion of the National Assessment of Educational Progress (NAEP) assessment; and various curriculum frameworks and blueprints including those by the American Association for the Advancement of Science and Goals 2000. All of these reform efforts have focused on schooling, and most have encompassed a variety of subject areas.

Less well-known in the educational literature are the parallel efforts of the informal education community in such locations as museums, television and radio studios, and community groups. Science and technology centers have led the way in transforming museums into hands- and minds-on learning centers by providing hands-on interactive programming and engaging patrons in a diverse array of activities (Association of Science and Technology Centers; Crane et al 1994; Falk and Dierking 1993 a and b). In addition, IMAX/OMNIMAX films have been created, and professional development and community and youth programs have become involved in informal education with youth of all ages as well as adults. This movement is particularly strong in science education, but these elements are shared across the forms of learning found in this work as well.

Education is increasingly pushed to consider itself as coupled (however loosely) to other sectors of society (Weick 1976, 1982). The school-to-work concept (whether formal partnerships or student career paths) and university/school collaborations provide two examples of this movement to consider education as a process in relationship to other organizations. Yet most educational researchers focus on the schools themselves: some at the macro level of school systems, others on individual schools, and yet others at classrooms or teaching practices.

Here, informal education has lessons to offer schools despite their apparent differences. Organizationally, schools are loosely coupled (if at all) with institutions such as museums, television studios, and community programs. Nonetheless, they share publics in common and there is much to be shared from one environment to the other. In this work, domestic violence shelters show the power and potential of feminist education in a setting very unlike public schools—but these educational practices *work* in shelters. That these practices work, and are effective, is important to know. Armed with the knowledge of effective practice, it becomes worthwhile to speculate the ways in which these kinds of education can be translated to, or connect with, public schooling.

Education on the Line

Is the Clothesline Project an educational method? It would seem, at minimum, to generate a reaction both from women who make shirts and persons of both sexes who view the shirts. Reaction, of course, does not equal learning. This is the difficulty of truly informal education: there is little way to gauge true effects on learning or understanding. The Clothesline Project concludes that it is an educational tool and one virtually unparalleled:

> As an educational medium, the Clothesline Project has few peers. It is the first public movement of its kind that links together the different forms of violence speaking to the quality of life all women have to live with in this culture. It brings viewers face to face with the painful and courageous stories of their neighbors, exposing a side of life that for too long has remained a silent and destructive force. Comments such as, "I could not speak for half an hour after viewing. I was moved, so horrified, so mad" are fre-

quent. Many express their disbelief: "I had no idea . . . no idea the problem was so widespread or that it could happen in our hometown." Frequently, the comments end with, "I am so sorry."

The Clothesline Project helps to underscore that feminist shelter pedagogy—the pedagogy of survival—is multidimensional, encompassing different learning styles and modalities, bringing together a concert of methods and resources to reach as many as possible. This text has variously argued that the feminist education that takes place in these domestic violence shelters is:

- A continuous process;
- Embedded in all shelter activities;
- Structured by a shelter environment with shared space, rules, and expectations;
- Conversational and dialogue-based;
- Reciprocal among staff and residents;
- Reliant on women's experiences, in which feminist content is infused;
- Conducted by other residents as well as staff;
- Reliant on both residents' and staff's engagement in the process;
- Nonlinear; and
- Woman-centered.

Each of these components is interconnected. The literature on feminist pedagogy focuses on the following elements: inclusion (e.g., representation in the curriculum and in class discussions); intimacy (e.g., use of small groups); voice (the sharing of stories and the use of authentic experiences in a pedagogical setting); authority/critiques of power (both of institutions and of classroom relationships, often resulting in different role expectations for both teachers and students); positionality (the recognition that we all speak and understand from multiple locations of gender, race, class, sexuality, and experiences); and mastery (the idea that material is to be explored rather than mastered, and that expertise is multidimensional) (Culley 1985; Gore 1992; Grumet 1988; Kenway and Modra 1992; Maher 1985, 1987; Maher and Tretrault 1994; Middleton 1993; Ropers-Huilman, 1998; Sattler 1996; Schniedewind 1987; Shrewsbury 1987; Weiler 1989). Here, I draw these two strands together in dialogue.

This type of learning seems dependent on the idea of feminist community, which regretfully has not been elaborated to any great extent within feminist writings on teaching. Here, shelters have a distinct advantage over university classrooms in their ordinariness, their nature as the space women occupy, whereas women must leave their spaces to come to a classroom. The learning process is disconnected from their overall experience, like the disjuncture between some theory and everyday living.

A second dimension, which is considered within the research on feminist teaching, is that of the unique context of each classroom or learning space. In shelters, this occurs whenever a woman enters or leaves shelter, because the dynamics shift. This is neither positive or negative; it simply is the case. Sometimes, it is the introduction of a new personality that causes the shift; other times it is the restructuring of power relationships among women in shelter because of an addition or subtraction. Race factors into this equation, as do level of need, number of children, age, health, and so on. The introduction of an HIV-positive woman into a shelter, for example, provoked heated debate among staff on the meaning of safety and confidentiality, concepts they took for granted when the topic was battering. Because this woman had obvious health needs, other residents discovered her HIV-positive status and this changed the nature of their relationships with each other and with her. Throughout this text, I have illustrated that these relationships are, in fact, part of the pedagogy of shelters, as women teach, and learn from, each other.

A professor in Ropers-Huilman's study relates a similar understanding of the dependency of a classroom environment on its constitutive individuals:

> The first thing is always understanding that what's going to [be] produced is changing. That is part of the sensitivity of who is in this particular group. How did this group of people come together this year in a way that is not like last year? How might, in this setting, this set of people feel empowered by some aspect of their own production? (1998, p. 50)

Leaving aside the problematic concept of empowerment, this dynamism, which crosses both environments, seems to represent and demand a particular flexibility of engagement on the part of teachers in both environments. In addition, where such flexibility exists, it would seem that the opportunity for student experiences to shape the curriculum is a reality.

If this is not education—the transformation of the ordinary into the extraordinary, and the creation of understanding and consciousness—then we cannot claim that knowledge is power, and education cannot entail the practice of freedom.

CHAPTER 6

Sisters Doin' It For Themselves

Free at last, free at last
Thank God almighty, I'm free at last.
Free at last, free at last
Thank God almighty, I'm free at last.
—African-American spiritual

Throughout time, whether we consider women in quilting circles, slaves sharing directions for the Underground Railroad, or women hanging shirts for the Clothesline Project, these actions include both an apparent effect and a deeper impact. The immediate, apparent effects are recognizable: women create friendships, slaves escape, and women tell their stories through shirts. The simplicity of these actions, however, belies the underlying changes necessary in order to take such action. Women do not simply begin to tell their stories; the dynamics of domestic violence ensure that they are mute. Slaves did not simply decide to escape; the pattern of ownership enslaved them as much as reality. In order for these simple, profound actions to take place, an enormous shift first occurs.

The Clothesline Project most openly demonstrates this shift. Recalling the women's descriptions of their own reactions to hanging the shirts, as well as the philosophy underpinning the Project itself, women create shirts *to take back power over their own lives.* Both consciousness-raising and woman-centered decision making in shelters deliberately attempt to create an atmosphere in which women both recognize their own power, and possess it, naming such actions empowerment.

The word *empowerment* is political, implying a current lack of power, or the need for a shift to a differential distribution of power; such is clearly the case among battered women. Ashcroft, a linguist, defines empowerment as "to bring into a certain condition or state . . . to bring into a state of ability/capacity to act" (1987, p. 143). On this basis, empowerment is suggested as a process that can be done either *for* or *by* an individual. "An empowered person, then, would be someone who believed in his or her abil-

79

ity/capability to act, and this belief would be accomplished by able/capable action. Since power has both capability and action components, the belief and resulting action are inseparable" (Ashcroft 1987, p. 143).

How does empowerment begin? Fostering empowerment in domestic violence shelters necessitates including women as decision makers and knowledge-generators because they are stakeholders in those decisions. Feminist education demands no less. Practice that would put women into the conversation about their lives requires that we view women differently, not as victims but as survivors and as reflective, thoughtful, capable peers. In so doing, the concept of emancipation from slavery, and of suffrage—having a vote in one's own life—are tantamount. Peter Easton adds,

> Education is a technology of participation. . . . Educators thus have a key role to play in bringing to social consciousness characteristics of given environments that impede learning, and in helping to design instructional components of strategies that will overcome these obstacles. (1989, p. 440)

Environments can be designed to impede participation or empowerment just as they impede learning. The politics of the domestic violence movement attempt to reverse the typical battered woman's experience, which is to have no power over her own life. At the shelters in this book, workers step away, asking women to do for themselves. Many women struggle and fight their way through shelter life for this same reason: used to having no power, they look to others for structure and guidance. The simple realization that "you get out of it what you put into it" carries profound significance to women claiming their own lives and taking responsibility for them, many able to do so for the first time. This chapter first examines what empowerment means in shelters, and then delves further into the ways in which shelters foster self-learning, peer learning, and group learning, each as a form of empowerment.

Fight for Power

Abusive relationships share a debilitating dynamic most often labeled "power and control." That is, the abuser takes all power in the relationship in order to control another person. The power may include controlling the finances; keeping the car keys; determining what friendships a woman may have; and all of the other small, day-to-day experiences that are hardly noticed—until they are gone. This dynamic contributes immeasurably to a woman's difficulty escaping. Sometimes, entering shelter represents the first decision, or act of power, that a woman has made in her own behalf.

Women enter shelter as an escape, not necessarily recognizing their need to regain power over their lives.

Shelter personnel, however, recognize that without the ability to make decisions and take responsibility, women will always need some type of help, rather than helping themselves. Both of the shelters I studied tried to reverse this pattern by immediately requiring women to make their own decisions, no matter how trivial; such practice, they believed, was necessary to assist women in regaining the power and control over their own lives. Further, both shelters assigned women regular chores and required them to care for their own children, to ensure that decisions were balanced with responsibility.

This engendering of independence is difficult both for staff and residents. It also seems oppositional to much of the "mothering" tone of some feminist literature on teaching (cf. Griffin 1992). Students of women faculty tend to place such faculty in parenting roles; as faculty, though, it is critical to be true parents in the sense that: "there are ways in which teaching is a little like parenting, that is you set something in motion but you simply can't control it. And that is, of course, exciting" (Ropers-Huilman 1998, p. 45). The picture in my mind is of learning to ride a bike. I begged my mother repeatedly to run down the street with me, guiding my bicycle as I "rode." She would run part-way down the street and then let go. I would then promptly fall off the bike and scrape my knees. Each time I wanted to "learn to ride," I begged her to help. Each time she would protest, but could be persuaded to run with me for a little while. One day, she would not run with me. That was the day that I scraped my knees very badly. That was also the day I learned to ride. Somewhere between recognizing women's needs to run with them and letting go of the bicycle is where teachers balance precariously as "parents" who let go.

This dynamic is worth examining from a number of perspectives. Staff have the advantage of seeing women over the long term—including those women who, when in shelter complain about the structure, living conditions, and the staff's appraisal of their problems but call back months or years later to speak to specific staffers. Their message is often, simply: "You were right. You said just what I needed to hear, but I just couldn't hear it then." Relatedly, bell hooks speaks of the time lag between students' experience of her classes and their realization that they have learned something. This is education as the practice of freedom. Hooks concurs: "this is one of the joys of education as the practice of freedom, for it allows students to assume responsibility for their choices" (1994, p. 19). However, if practiced as "one-size-fits-all" education, the liberation is lost for some. For these women in shelter—the ones who "make it"—taking back control over their own lives and decisions is one of the most painful, difficult aspects of reclaiming freedom.

During the day, women are asked to perform frightening tasks at shelters, including filing civil protection orders.[1] They also are asked to meet their own needs, with some assistance, for things such as food, clothing, housing, employment, and child care. Although counselors and shelter staff provide guidance, it is largely the women themselves who navigate the system. Their struggle is conveyed to other women in living room conversations, where word-of-mouth is a powerful force to recommend one job program over another, or to find child care. Most of these women face several primary needs: child care; employment; housing; and, for some, education or training. Many take preliminary steps toward these goals, such as applying for Aid to Families with Dependent Children (AFDC) and food stamps to eke out a living before they find employment or while they enter training programs that will help them to find jobs. Importantly, these women take these steps themselves, but not alone.

Making (Difficult) Choices

Women's choices encompass much more than whether or not to leave her partner. Painfully, these choices take the form of quotidian affairs: Will she file charges? Will she go on public assistance (food stamps, AFDC, welfare)? Will she file for Section 8 (public) housing? Who can she let know she's in shelter and safe? Who will care for her children while she looks for work? How will she arrange for transportation? What forms must she file to be eligible for programs? How will she dress her child? And so forth. In one of the two shelters, residents meet with staff and develop goals (e.g., getting a job) as well as a rough outline of how to accomplish those goals. Resources (telephone numbers, forms, bus tokens) are provided, and the staff member periodically checks on the resident's progress toward the goals but does not intervene unless a situation becomes dangerous. In this way, residents make their own passage through the social service system and struggle toward normalcy in their lives. Even in the other shelter, which is more directive (e.g., women must agree to enter a shelter-based counseling program and must meet regularly, generally on a weekly basis, with a case manager who tracks their progress), women are largely expected to sort through options and make their own way toward new lives.

---

1. In Washington, D.C., the woman who files a CPO is herself responsible either for serving the papers on her abuser or for making arrangements for the abuser to be served. Either way, it is not a safe activity.

In feminist pedagogical terms, Maher and Tretrault would define this process as "making students responsible for their own learning" (1994, p. 20). However, they pose this in opposition to the exercise of professorial authority. I disagree; it seems that the person in authority (either the professor or the shelter worker) retains the power to choose whether to retain or extend her authority, and as Nick Burbles reminds us, what is extended can be withdrawn. Some respond well to this system, which some shelters regard as part of their mission of feminist empowerment. Some residents don't respond well at all; these residents seem to require more structure. The reason I make this point is that many shelter residents feel that they are forced to make choices about their lives (to go on welfare or food stamps; to rent an apartment; to look for a job; to find child care) with inadequate resources or information. Largely, these women want someone in authority to tell them what to do, while the position of the shelter workers, here and elsewhere, is that women who have been abused have had little or no control over their lives, and need to regain that control by making their own decisions in order to live independently. Both perspectives are important: the women feel they need more support to make the "right" choices, for their own good; the shelter workers feel the women need to make their own choices, for their own good. From either perspective, though, the transition of power is not a simple, one-way, unproblematic transaction between "teacher" and "student." One interesting dynamic in shelters results from the dual identity of some workers as both workers and formerly battered women. As the latter, they are "successful"; that is, they didn't return to their abusers, or if they did, they escaped eventually. Most escaped via shelters (in some cases, the very shelter in which they work). These successes may result in less flexibility in shelters based on the belief that structures successful for them should then be maintained as is, and they will be successful for more women.

As they take on the task of reclaiming freedom, women critique the system; as painful and complex as this process is, few women are uniformly positive. However, in doing so they also reclaim their voice. Weiss and Friedman (1995) conclude that voice is the basis for successful feminist communities: "It seems clear from the literature on feminist communities that among the most successful are those that are based on and address women's self-defined needs and that build in ways to keep women's voices at the center." (pp. 13–14) Yet as Iris Marion Young describes, community can by definition be exclusive:

> In ordinary speech for most people in the U.S., the term community refers to the people with whom I identify in a locale. It refers to neighborhood, church, schools. It also carries connotations of

ethnicity or race. For most people in the U.S., insofar as they consider themselves members of communities at all, a community is a group that shares a specific heritage, a common self-identification, a common culture and set of norms. (1986/1995, p. 244)

If there is anything absent from shelter "curriculum," it is a lost opportunity to problematize race. Shelters are sites of conflict, and some conflicts get acted out as race issues. However, they are not dealt with as such. It is hard to say whether this is too much to ask. All the other forms of shelter pedagogy are linked directly to domestic violence or the skills women need to be self-sufficient. Yet this—a conscious effort to ally across race, not only in terms of domestic violence experiences—might assist women in the longer term. As one shelter director said, if we could get past the "us versus them" equation, would it be easier to deal with women versus men?

In one shelter, women of all ages and races worked together and shared their stories. Further, these women were diversely classed—some were college graduates with careers, while others were destitute. Here, all voices seemed to be heard. In contrast, at the other shelter, the majority of residents were African American and low-income. Here, when a new resident of a different race (the most prominent was Latina) entered, there was a sense of a closed group, akin to a high school clique, of which the new resident was not a member. This was occasionally exacerbated by language, as the following story illustrates:

I had come to the shelter to interview another woman for the study. I sat down in the living room to review my notes and make preparations. I had barely seated myself when a young child flung herself into my lap, clutching a book. It was one of the "Goosebumps" series, popular among pre-teens. I assumed that she wanted me to read to her; then I realized that Angelica spoke only Spanish, as did her mother. As Angelica continued to bring me books her mother and I had a halting conversation, utilizing my high-school mastery of Spanish. Then she asked me for help. She wanted to make a telephone call—a collect call to a professor. She handed me a 1-900 number and I found myself unable to help, unable to communicate, unable to even begin to explain what was wrong with the telephone number. After long conversations with multiple telephone operators, other crisis hotlines, and my conscience, I realized that Gloria's silence was almost absolute. She had left her partner (su esposa) in Texas (Tejas) to seek help—yet here she was, in a shelter far from home, with a volunteer unable to help with a simple request. It was even later when I realized that

in the Spanish I had used, I had chosen the familiar tú *rather than*
*the more proper—and appropriate—*usted.

During this interaction, other residents continued to wander into the room
where Gloria, Angelica, and I were sitting. They shrugged their shoulders,
commenting "none of us can talk to her." With the exception of one bilin-
gual staffer, this woman and her child were linguistically isolated, unable to
gain the power of collective consciousness by comparing their stories with
those of the other residents. This is an important interrogation of the definition of "community" within these feminist shelters. With these noted exceptions, a dialogue about cross-cultural communication is missing. Shelters
place their emphasis on commonality rather than difference and on the
dynamics of women versus men rather than women together. In part this
constitutes recognition of women's lives and the love they have for their
partners and male children. It also arises in part out of fear of accusations of
shelters as bastions of lesbianism, accusations that unfortunately can dam-
age the shelter's relationship with the community upon which it is dependent for funding.

These two shelters are critical of existing power relations in which certain groups are advantaged and others are disadvantaged. In accordance
with their missions, they have chosen to focus on the social structures that
reinforce the domination of men as a group over women as a group and to
provide a space for women to speak and revision their futures. Feminism
calls for the inclusion of these absent voices; shelters try to legitimate and
structure this process for their residents. In so doing, Patricia Hill Collins
and bell hooks would remind them that "voice" tends to mean a white, middle-class woman's voice (Hill Collins 1990; hooks 1984). Voice is not
merely the sound of women talking. In shelters, voice encompasses the ability and willingness to speak aloud and the reassurance that women will be
heard across race, class, and ethnic boundaries.

A Contrast in Control

While analyzing these women's stories and struggling with the concepts of
how to write about teaching and learning in a space that is not considered
educational, I began some government-sponsored research on correctional
education. My first thought was that this might give me some insight on
shelter education; after all, inmates shared a number of characteristics with
these women. As it happens, though, prison education is much more "classical" than it might seem: within prisons, education looks the way that it
looks in our classrooms (ironies aside). Students enroll in classes, with curriculum, assessments, and a recognizable framework of educational bureau-

cracy. Prisoners, like students—or should I write, students, like prison-ers?—are subject to a high level of surveillance (Foucault, 1962, 1975, 1977). I did not find the kind of similarity that I'd hoped for. However, what I did find was the power of contrast. Shelters *could* be much like pris-ons. They *could* confine women (for their own safety provides reason or excuse enough). They *could* make choices for women (since some would argue these women have a history of choosing badly for themselves). They *could* subject women to a structured curriculum on the cycle of violence, safety planning, characteristics of batterers, and many other topics. They *could* assess women's performance based on a set of preordained criteria (since the space in shelters must be reserved for those who need it most).

The shelters I know do none of these things. That, in essence, describes their radical venture, in which they take women in as former prisoners of war, refugees, and surround them with just enough structure to place them in proximity to other women with similar stories, resources they can use, and knowledge that is useful to them. And then, in truly radical style, they step back and let these women decide whether and when to use these fea-tures to their advantage.

Education as the practice of freedom—the kind of education that con-fronts this frustrating situation head-on and acknowledges that even when women make choices we might not make, or see as wrong, they have the right and responsibility to make their own choices—has been a theme throughout this work. As other chapters show, however, when women identify their own shelter-based learning it is in more concrete terms, that is, skills (I learned to cook) or triumphs (I got custody of my child). Can this kind of learning be de-emphasized in shelters? Should it be downplayed? It is part of the explicit teaching mission—and it is visibly enacted by women in shelters. For these women, learning is visible and empowerment is abstract, but both are necessary. The weak point is the juncture where women who require more structure, feeling themselves incapable of taking up the task of reconstituting their lives, encounter such a pedagogy of self-actualization.

Women in shelter challenge rules, and the absence of rules; structure, and its lack. Women wrestling with defining themselves sometimes cry out for assistance and find they must rely on themselves. Women seeking absolute freedom find themselves faced with responsibility. Child care illus-trates the clash between some women's habits and shelter policies. For example, women often ask other women to watch their children while they run an errand, apply for food stamps, or perform duties in the shelter. Despite the availability of other willing women, many shelters do not allow this practice. Where it is allowed, it is carefully regulated; in one shelter, res-idents must sign an agreement to care for another person's child and must specify the period of time for the agreement. Shelters view such responsibility as part of building responsible parenting practices, as well as a "reality check." It forces women to deal with the issue of how they can enter the work force, and provide for their children, successfully. Mary, a resident with a first-grade son, talks about this problem:

> Res.: *We need to have some parenting classes and we need like a daycare or aftercare—even more so aftercare than daycare.*
>
> Int.: *What for?*
>
> Res.: *For the kids, like when they come from school and their parents are in school, too, and they, you know, have somewhere that they can go. Aftercare, I have to pay $100.00 out of my Social Security check because I get out of school at 4:00 and he gets out of school at 3:15 and he can't come here without me being here because there's no one, you know, to watch him, to supervise him. So I have to pay the school $100.00 a month.*
>
> Int.: *So you'd like after school services for him?*
>
> Res.: *Yeah, because you know, I might not be here but you know, the next person—because everybody might not be able to have $100.00 a month to pay.*

Given the truly longitudinal picture of women's struggles in shelter, I side with the shelters' position to push, gently but firmly, for these women to lead their own lives. Learning is a struggle—and after all, as Emma Goldman reportedly said, "The revolution will not be televised."

Yet on a shorter timeline, such policies seem insensitive, even harsh, like exposing an arachnaphobe to a room full of spiders. I have, however, viewed times when women re-created the same relationships of dependency that they had with their partners, only this time using shelter workers. Here, I believe, shelters provide an example of where theory must meet reality; ideas about women making their own choices—including nonaction—clash with shelters' goals to have women choose action of some kind. Theories about being supportive and nurturing in safe spaces, which some feminist research espouses, must meet the reality of the need to create women who are self-supporting and self-nurturing, on their own.

A Place to Call Home

Housing is the issue most consistently brought up by women, although child care follows quickly on its heels. The struggle for housing is different by the region of the country where women live. In Florida, Section 8 housing was difficult, but not impossible, to find. In Washington, D.C., residents can struggle for months, applying and being rejected either for their Section 8, or by the housing where they have applied.

> Int.: What's the most important thing right now to do or get figured out?
> Res.: The most important thing?
> Int.: Yeah.
> Res.: In my life right now?
> Int.: Yeah.
> Res.: Is to get me and [my son] a home.
> Int.: Yeah?
> Res.: Yeah. And then from there I can accomplish my other things because I'd have a room to sit down under a table with a light. That's all it is.

These details imply that the idea of a future of their own design is firmly rooted.

Housing is not a pleasant topic for these women. They encounter rats, and worse, when they visit housing they can afford on public assistance. I look at their young children and shudder at the thought. Yet they persevere—many with the barest of scaffolding support from the shelter personnel. In Washington, D.C., the intricacies of the public housing program are well-known on the street. Some women learned of options from other homeless men and women they met prior to coming to shelter. In the following narrative, Mary explains the process she went through to find out about housing. Her story is typical of the shelter process:

> Int.: So where are you going to go after you're through here?
> Res.: I hope I find an apartment and continue school. I registered for Saturday college.
> Int.: What's that?
> Res.: A college course you could take on Saturdays. It's free.
> Int.: What are you going to take?
> Res.: Physical therapy.
> Int.: Who offers that?
> Res.: The government. Anybody can go. You can go, you all can go. It's free.
> Int.: How did you find out about that?
> Res.: From here [shelter].
> Int.: Did [your social worker] tell you?
> Res.: No, [another shelter worker] told me. Do you want me to get the paper for you and show you?

Int.: *Maybe in a minute. Tell me how this works. You're just talking about getting your GED and——overhears you and she says hey, you should check this out?*

Res.: Yeah. [The program counselor], she brought them here, brought a stack of the pamphlets here and I picked it up and [two other shelter workers] told me the rest about it.

Int.: *So you were already enrolled in GED and you just—you found this information and then you asked somebody more?*

Res.: Uh-huh, but they told me about going to school at [a government service office].

Int.: *And they told you about [Section 8 housing]?*

Res.: National Capitol Housing, but I had already went down there before I came here. Then when I got [to shelter], they did tell me I could go down there and—

Int.: *They gave you a letter or something that gave you priority?*

Res.: Yeah. They gave me a letter stating that I am a resident of [the shelter] and they—also they give me vouchers for clothes, clothing.

Other women learn as they go. Consider this statement from a shelter worker on how she teaches women to rely on other women rather than on men:

Staff: *I talk to them also about surviving out there far as jobs. Talk to them about you know how they have to sell themself sometimes you know. You have to, when I say sell, you know a lot of women come in there and they want to talk about how do I get a place you know. And I tell that they have a lot of apartment complexes that have their own in-house section 8's and if you go and find out and talk with the people, rental office, and talk with people, resident managers, that its like selling yourself and you have to talk to someone because they, you don't that person right there is the person could help you, you know. A lot time we so eager, we don't, we always, kinda say we are the first one jumping in talking, howling for men for help. We don't want to talk to a woman and see if a woman would help us, you know. And I tell them that you know. Why don't you talk to a woman. We always, we [are] so eager to talk to men you know (laughing).*

The lesson here is simple: there are people who can, and will, help you. You're not alone. And, you're welcome to be here, in shelter, while you need that help. This lesson is believed, as well as offered. Current and former residents refer to shelter as home. They miss shelter, for its atmosphere as well as the staff they had grown close to. They keep the friends they made among the women who were in shelter at the same time.

(Re)Building Trust

Yet pragmatic, everyday knowledge, while necessary, is not sufficient for women to envision the future. Women and their children look over their shoulders and see the shadow of the other, the men in their lives who have hurt them and whom they in many cases still love. They believed in themselves, the relationship, and their partner—but were betrayed. Slaves built relationships with their masters and masters' families, only to be separated and sold. Thus, their belief in others often is weakened, if not absent. They trusted in things that have not held up over time. Therefore, from the time that a woman enters shelter as a resident, the operating question is, "what next?" The implication underlying the question is, "what's real, what's trustworthy, what's safe to believe in?" Staff and residents alike feel pressured by these constraints to find and organize a plan for each woman that enables her to move on to a violence-free life outside of the shelter. Fundamental to this planning is learning to trust workers and the shelter system.

Shelter workers recognize that before they can help these women, the women must trust them. This trust is the first step in a long healing process, and doesn't all come at once. The following narrative describes this process:

> *I mean, people come in here most of the time, they don't trust anyone. They don't trust. You know, and you don't know what's going on in their life. If you don't find out some of those small details, you're in a lot of trouble because you're not going to do nothing but get people in here just coming through the system and going out and having no substance. You know, you've got to [get] down to the nitty gritty. That's what happens when you talk to them. Things come up, unfold—you know, their life unfolds. They've been hurt from their children. You know, some of that stuff is horrible; most of the stuff is horrible. Women have been through a lot, a whole lot of stuff.*

These experiences of both women and residents become part of an ongoing conversation, across residents and across staff, about survival, solutions, and success. These conversations are held in a variety of ways—through individual talks, through group sessions, informally in an office or a hall-way, or in response to a comment or behavior. The learning community of shelters functions as an extended family, where these conversations are embedded in the everyday lives of women working toward survival. Staff form a kind of family, mothers and sisters, surrounding the shelter residents. As family members do, staff take on different roles: some are mother figures, some are "big sisters," giving tough love; others take the position of being just like the residents, only once removed. This pseudo-family is amazingly successful, and in part this success is based on acknowledging, yet looking deeper into, the problems presented by residents. As one staffer explains:

> *Staff:*   *[Consider what it's like,] following someone through the whole process. You take the phone call, you do the screening, you do intake and all along the way, who that person is and what their issues really are and what really brought them into the shelter and what are, you know, the presenting problem as opposed to the real issues are always very different. The real issues are always very different from the presenting problem, so learning how to discern what the underlying issues are going to be sooner rather than later.*

> *Staff:*   *Everybody comes in there always saying I know what I want. I want to get my own place. I want to get a job. I want to go to school and everyone says the same thing. And I told people every time they come in, I am not a type of person that too much listens to your talk, I said, I watch you. And I said and I said if you're walking, you're talking, then you want something. When you're talking something and walking a different line, something's wrong, you know. So, you'll see a person come in there and they meet with you and they talk with you and they ask you a bunch of questions about, you know, how can I do this, like go to school or what would be the best training for me or, you know, every last one of them say that, you know, and it's real hard to say who will be the person that will go and do that, you know. Because even the ones that start out that way, still end up either not going through with it or leaving.*

Staff delve into these levels of awareness, while recognizing that women do go through stages while in shelter (Griffin 1992).

This constant cycle of learning and teaching, of testing the edges of how far they have come as survivors, is a continuous undercurrent of shelter work. In the words of one worker, change is inevitable:

> *Staff:*   *When a staff person starts, when I'm interviewing some-*
> *one or we do a hire, I sit with her and I go over staff proce-*
> *dures and I sit and I look at her and I think, you know, in*
> *six months, you're going to be a changed person and you*
> *don't even know it.*

The cyclical process of education means that things are in constant flux within shelters. Workers are learning, and residents are learning. Residents learn because of staff and in spite of them. Most residents, though, credit shelter staff with much of their success, including their ability to tell and live with their stories.

CHAPTER 7

Teaching to Transcend

A few more beatings of the wind and rain,
Ere the winter will be over . . .
—Negro spiritual and slave song

Live Free or Die
—Harriet Tubman and Frederick Douglass

Women must translate knowledge into power to *practice* freedom. Perhaps the most central aspect of this transfer from learning to practice is the ability to envision a future. Caught up in their fragmented lives of survival, neither slaves nor battered women imagine much of a future beyond the next hour, the next day, the next week. In fact, battered women have an additional incentive for *not* looking forward to the future. As many describe during the second stage of the cycle of violence, the "tension-building phase," they "walk on eggshells," trying not to disturb the fragile peace, yet know from experience that an explosion is inevitable. They often flee because they realize, or fear, that there will be no future—that they will die (because an abuser has threatened to kill them) or because the abuse has touched their children in some way (either through physical abuse, emotional abuse, or the effects of watching their mother battered). These realizations, that any future at all is hinged on escape, can lead women to shelter. However, most still lack a vision of a concrete future. If they do have a vision of that future, it is one without abuse—but also without detail. Shelter workers confront the challenge of moving women from consciousness to action.

Many women in shelter face, for the first time, the reality that they have not had a vote in their lives, or their futures. Their conversations reveal tentative steps toward picturing their own realities. Women in shelter experience a change from escaping violence to shelter learning to planning for

93

the future.[1] Yet at the same time as women gain the skills they need to survive, they are most likely to be destroyed. It is a fact that women who leave their abusive partners are the most likely to be killed by those partners either during or immediately after their escape (Bart and Moran 1993; Berry 1996; Ford Foundation 1992). Domestic violence is largely about power and control; in typical arguments that education is power, we overlook the very real, very strong oppositional (and in this case, violent) force against women's education and empowerment. Shelters are designed to be subversive, in offering women tools to protect themselves from the opposition that comes from within, as well as from external violence.

Women flee with the clothes on their backs and the backs of their children. They enter shelter, sometimes in the dead of night, with exhausted dreams and unimaginable realities. Once in shelter, others meet women's basic needs, but women themselves must struggle through the process of empowerment with the assistance of their peers. Empowerment cannot simply be measured in terms of women speaking aloud, no matter how powerful. Empowerment cannot simply be measured in terms of women's learning, no matter how necessary or impressive. Empowerment must be measured by whether women survive, whether the process of empowerment truly assists women in gaining the skills, knowledge, power, and determination they need to move ahead. Empowerment is designed to help women gain the kinds of knowledge they need to understand that they are not alone in their trouble, to move forward with their lives, and perhaps to hope and to dream again. Shelters foster dreams, but they emphasize survival.

The Meaning of Survival

What does survival mean to these women, many of whom fled fearing for their lives? What does tomorrow look like? As described later in this chapter, women's needs differ at various stages in shelter experience. Here, I paint a picture of what is for many the most meaningful knowledge, what they need for survival—knowledge about how to live in the world. By this I mean many things: how to write a resumé, apply for a job, deal with children's emotions about their fathers, interpret child custody laws, find housing, file for divorce. These tasks should not be reduced to simple life skills, because they are a piece of a much larger, feminist education agenda in

---

1. At the same time, this work acknowledges that many women return to their abusers multiple times, residing in shelters in between their relationships before they leave their abusive partners. Other women do not leave their partners. Still others feel emancipated, leave their partners, and are killed. These experiences provide a complex interplay of the realities, and danger, of knowledge.

which women come to see their own power and take hold of their lives through self-learning, peer learning, and group learning. This learning takes place both between residents, and between residents and staff at the shelters in this study. The practical education women receive in shelters includes child rearing techniques and basic housekeeping. The demystification of expertise is the operating philosophy in domestic violence shelters. At the same time, the responsibilities that women are given in shelter accomplish two things beyond either empowerment or educational goals: (1) they provide a context for women to interact with each other over common tasks; and (2) they distract, while still building toward, the all-too-intense struggle for safety, stability, and less worrisome lives.

Shelter education contains an inherent duality: it is at once inward- and outward-focused. The outward focus is on skills. The inward focus, begun with consciousness-raising and self-reliance, is continued with a focus on positive self-regard, defined by staff as managing the inward confusion and cacaphony that often results from abusive situations. Each of the staff members, although taking specific approaches (e.g., the mother figure) focuses on the interaction between internal and external needs. As one counselor relates,

> Staff: *Battered women are not only battered, they have other issues and sometimes we have to get through the other issues in order to get to the battering. And in the meantime, you've got to be nurturing them, you know, and making them feel like they can trust, you know, and it's just really something to do that I feel wonderful doing. I do.*

In general, residents find this atmosphere helpful:

> *It's nice. It's teaching me a lot. I'm learning to be a better person. Like, I never cooked; now I cook, and clean up. I wash the dishes. Now I do a lot of things. I do like if they need the basement cleaned, I always volunteered.*

> Int.: *If you had to say what services that you've gotten here besides food and shelter what would you say?*
> Res.: *Honestly, the chance to just settle down. I think a lot of people take for granted the peace that you get here. Just the simplicity of knowing that you have one or two chores to do. You know you don't have to come in cook, clean up, bathe your kids, get yourself together and go through all the rigmarole. I get to go in, make a plate, sit down and eat and all I have to do tonight is clean out the refrigera-*

tor. I thinks that [is] one thing that a lot of people take for
granted, but I know what it is like to have to try to do it all
in a minimal amount of time.

As I write this I am overwhelmed by the fragility of these women's stories. They were told to me, not as they are told to each other, but as a writer
who would bring them to the world. What an awesome responsibility. They
are garish in the harsh light of day. These interviews were taped in a children's playroom, ironically in the midst of toys and soft dolls given to the
shelter to comfort its smallest residents. Residents being interviewed often
would pick up a rattle, or a toy—or would have their children with them to
mitigate the harshness of their speech. Reading them, I am overwhelmed by
the power, the sadness, the hope, and the singular focus on survival.

Women define survival differently at different stages in their shelter
experience. These stages became even clearer through a coincidence of the
study: when a tape failed to record, I reinterviewed a resident several weeks
after her initial interview. It was, in the words of one interviewer, as though
we had interviewed a totally different woman. As new entrants, women
focus inwardly, on care of basic needs:

Staff: *When a woman first comes, probably we have our own*
           honeymoon period. They are so grateful, they feel like
           they've been rescued in a certain sense and they're just
           happy to be out of the situation and happy to be with us.
           Usually that's accompanied by a recovery period, just time
           to chill. And they begin to talk with other residents. What
           sometimes happens after that is a period of real intense
           anger at us for not being able to totally save them. Sort of
           like, thank you for saving me and why the hell didn't you
           save me better or more or all the way.

           Because unfortunately, significant change is always
           going to be difficult. It's not going to come easy. And
           when they come to us . . . the more change they're able to
           go through, the more successful we've been and the more
           painful it's going to be for them. They're going to have to
           go through some kind of process and usually the sort of
           first process they go through is understanding and getting
           with the fact that we're not going to fix it all for them,
           they've got to do it themselves.

As more established residents, women diversify their activities, and in so
doing they struggle both inwardly and outwardly. New possibilities appear
throughout the 'life course' of women entering, residing, and leaving shel-

ter, as their lives change in significant ways. Recall Maslow's hierarchy; you can't self-actualize without food in your stomach. For more established residents, needs move further up the hierarchy:

> *Res.:* To me survival is probably just an emotional state. One when I can be at peace with the things that have gone on and be comfortable emotionally. It's really rough 'cause sometimes you have thoughts of wanting to do harm to your abuser and you don't want bad things to happen . . . you know, just a state of being at peace with what's gone on and my moving on, basically is survival to me.
>
> *Int.:* Moving on.
>
> *Res.:* Emotionally, you know just the hate and the hurt. Just all the different changes you go through.
>
> *Int.:* How are you going to get there?
>
> *Res.:* I am almost there. I used to sit and think of these elaborate plans of what to do, and I don't do that anymore, and he doesn't bother me anymore. You know just the thought of him. I am still scared. I am still very very hurt, but I am not at a point where I used to blame myself and feel like it was something that I caused. I feel like it was something that I allowed to go on, but I don't feel like it was something that I caused or made happen. I write a lot, every day.
>
> *Int.:* A journal?
>
> *Res.:* Yes. When you go back it is one thing to give thought to something, but it is another thing to read it and to know that they were your words and your thoughts. And just sometimes if I feel whatever is affecting me I just try to chill out and think it through and try to figure out is it a cause of something that happened or just something I am feeling right now.

At this stage, the shelter's goal is transformation—transformation of low confidence into invincibility; transformation of low efficacy into high efficacy; transformation of self-blame into understanding and self-actualization; and transformation of violence into nonviolence and hope. Slowly, these types of learning bridge the way to shouldering the responsibility for women's own, genuine survival for themselves and their children. In real terms, this is education as the practice of freedom at its most fundamental level.

An Unbroken Circle

When I began this work, little did I realize the extent to which women flee-ing domestic violence literally as well as metaphorically resembled the escape of slaves. Jacqueline Tobin and Raymond Dobard provide the last, critical link. Their work, *Hidden in Plain View*, posits that not only did par-ticular patterned quilts hung outside send signals to slaves but that the quilts themselves were a complex code of directions, advice, and even topographi-cal maps. As they write, "the Quilt Code is a mystery-laden, secret commu-nication system of employing quiltmaking terminology as a message map for black slaves escaping on the underground railroad" (1999, p. 3). Indeed, Harriet Tubman herself was a quilter.

The importance of this last link to the parallel between the Underground Railroad and domestic violence shelters illustrates the power of the ordinary, as well as the multilayered meanings and covert social protest that can be inherent in regular activities. They ask, "Why were quilts the chosen medium to conceal and yet reveal a means of escape? How would an enslaved people who had little knowledge, if any, of the land beyond the plantation be able to chart a path out of bondage?" (1999, p. 27).

Women's experiences provide one answer. *The Quilters*, a play linking the experiences of women during the westward movement to quilt patterns provides evidence that a community would understand its own symbols; for example, the abstract line pattern known as the "log cabin" quilt would immediately elicit understanding—and a common bond. Tobin and Dobard agree, writing that "patchwork quilts were readable objects in nineteenth-century America" (1999, p. 28). As Aiken writes about pincushions, Tobin and Dobard provide a parallel, arguing that "some quilts served as bill-boards or banners for women to express their social or moral convictions through the names and meanings they gave the patterns" (1999, p. 28). "Familiarity provides the perfect cover. Messages can be skillfully passed on through objects that are are seen so often they become invisible" (1999, p. 35). Shelters strive for precisely this invisibility. Another setting Tobin and Dobard link with slave uprisings is the black churches, where slaves would plan escapes under the guise of praising God. Many spirituals have been reinterpreted in the light of such secretive communication, as this text has attempted to reinterpret some of women's traditions in a similar light.

In the excitement of finding such concrete evidence of the hidden mean-ings in ordinary materials, we must not forget their utilitarian origins. Quilts originated as a way to keep warm and to use scraps of material. Quilting circles originated as a way of teaching and learning quilting as well as creating community. Quilting—and escape—arose out of necessity. In this way, remembering all the levels of meaning, we may examine domestic violence shelters as the latest in the chain of such social protest and action, "hidden in plain sight."

The slave quilt underscores another point made earlier in this text: slaves, and women, are not rescued; they rescue themselves. "The African slave, despite the horrors of the Middle Passage, did not sail to the New World alone. These African slaves brought with them their metaphysical systems, their languages, their terms for order and their expressive cultural practices which even the horrendous Middle Passage and the brutality of everyday life on the plantation could not effectively obliterate" (Henry Louis Gates, quoted in *Hidden in Plain Sight*).

These quilt codes, together with songs and other mnemonic devices created by slaves, assisted escaping slaves in finding stations on the Underground Railroad. Domestic violence shelters similarly began as a network of safe houses to which women were directed in secret. Shelters maintain this secrecy today by providing partial directions, by requesting that women keep shelter names and telephone numbers separate, by maintaining secret addresses, and through a system of checks of a women's authenticity or true need for shelter (screening for potential infiltrators, such as the unsympathetic sister of an abuser). Frederick Douglass himself commented on the necessity of silence: "I hated the secrecy, but where slavery is powerful, and liberty is weak, the latter is driven to concealment or to destruction" (Frederick Douglass quoted in *Hidden in Plain Sight*, p. 137).

Yet there is solidarity in silence. Glaspell's women exercise silent complicity with the woman who murdered her husband. The network known as Jane provided confidentiality regarding abortion. And as Tobin and Dobard continue, "This need for secrecy is understandable when we consider that from the time of slavery until today secrecy was one way the black community could protect itself. If the white man didn't know what was going on, he couldn't seek reprisals. Secrecy appears to be wedded to protection . . . you do not tell strangers what is kept sacred to the family" (1999, p. 123). For domestic violence shelters, protection can only be maintained by such secrecy.

Slave quilts provide yet another parallel to women's escape. Tobin and Dobard write that nine quilts would have been displayed in succession, each one telling the slaves to prepare a little bit more. For example, the first quilt they describe is the monkey wrench pattern, which they argue would have let slaves know to begin gathering the tools they would need. A second quilt would display the wagon wheel, indicating another step in the process. Escapes were planned carefully, step by step. The existence of severe reprisals, including death, cautioned slaves to leave nothing to chance.

Similarly, women prepare to leave their partners bit by bit, often entering and leaving shelter several times in the process. Women, too, plan their escapes with extreme caution, fearing for their lives. The existence of severe reprisals, including death, cautions women to leave nothing to chance. Women's positions as mothers, wives, girlfriends, and significant others complicate such partings. Unlike slaves, who with few exceptions did not link themselves emotionally to their masters, women bear the brunt of this extra dimension. Slaves faced a fairly constant condition of deprivation; women become tormented by the occasional affection, and sparks of hope.

Some women, faced with the reality of what it takes to survive on their own, see no option but to return, and part of the philosophy of empowerment is letting go. Education as the practice of freedom—the kind of education that confronts this frustrating situation head-on—acknowledges that even when women make choices we might not make, or see as wrong, they have the right and responsibility to make their own choices.

In keeping with the slave quilt parallel, shelters are one of women's tools, the "monkey wrench" of the slave quilt. However, shelters are as limited as they are radical. Earlier references have been made to the time limits placed on how long a woman may remain in shelter. There are other limits, less structurally bounded than they are products of the violent relationship itself. Shelters provide tools, not solutions. At best they are, like the Underground Railroad, way stations on the way to freedom. Shelters are the emergency room of the women's movement, not hospitals nor long-term care facilities. Women's processes of leaving present challenges to shelters that slaves—often more single-minded in their escape—would not have. Shelters want so desperately to help. Surely Harriet Tubman felt some of these same emotions when she tried to rescue her parents, only to find that they would not come. A staffer talks about the patience she has learned as part of shelter work and education:

> *Staff:* *It takes a tremendous amount of patience and tolerance if you're a radical feminist to deal with domestic violence because . . . often you're nothing more than a band-aid, helping a woman get bandaged up and go back to the situation. You have to accept the fact that she might need to leave three or six times before she leaves for good. She might never leave for good. In some cases, the most you're going to hope for is that she's going to understand a little bit more of some things but not really make a fundamental change. So, it can be really frustrating and it's sometimes difficult.*

Another staffer speaks of this process not in terms of patience, but that of faith:

> *Staff:*   *I do know that it's a basic faith and belief and understand-*
> *ing that . . . all of life is a path and you can only go one step*
> *at a time and everybody is where they're supposed to be*
> *right now . . . also, I don't consider it a failure when some-*
> *body goes back. I consider that they've been with us for as*
> *long as they've been with us, they've gotten what they*
> *were ready to get, what we were able to give and that's*
> *better than nothing. And if they need to be back, they will*
> *and if they need to stay where they are for the rest of their*
> *lives, that's their life path, you know.*
>
>   *So, it does take a certain amount of faith in the good-*
> *ness of life or the rightness of life, you know. But it's really*
> *wonderful to know that in some small way, there's been*
> *some effect. To be able to be there for somebody who's*
> *coming to you and then going back out there and then*
> *three months later they call you because they're having a*
> *problem dealing or a year later they're back. And they*
> *knew all that time that you were going to be there for them*
> *and not chastise them for having gone back or whatever*
> *and accept that. And that's a special gift to be able to give.*

Fundamentally, shelters and their pedagogy challenge residents and staff alike, and both are caught up in the continuous learning cycle. Staff know women's issues are inextricably bound together, as are women, workers, and residents. Their survival is intertwined. "It is a story of secrets, involving routes and language, codes and music. It is, in the end, a story of triumph and freedom, bought at great price . . ." (1999, p. 54). The musical *Fiddler on the Roof*, which I saw as a child, impressed me with one line that I have remembered since then: children need both roots and wings. Wings—the symbol of freedom—reoccur on slave quilts, and so shelters structure women's environments to provide both roots and wings, recognizing that each is necessary to survive.

> *There's a river of birds*
> *in migration—*
> *a nation*
> *of women with wings.*

Appendix A

The Dynamics of Domestic Violence

Domestic violence[1] is virtually invisible. One of the most insidious facts about domestic violence is its secrecy; although thousands of women die each year at the hands of their abusers—the men they loved—these acts are shielded by the division between public and private spheres. The division between public and private (often referred to as the men's sphere and women's sphere, or separate spheres) has clear historical origins that mark it as fundamentally power-based and political; despite the changes in social structure from the time of its origin to the present day, the concept is still current in arguments over the right to privacy, sex education, and the provision of social services and social surveillance. The division originally stemmed from the time of the industrial revolution, when men left home to work (in industry rather than farming) and women, particularly those in the middle class, were encouraged to stay home, safeguarding the home and serving as a moral agent. Women became exemplars of the moral high ground, and as such were considered to need seclusion, away from the morally questionable world outside the home; that is, men left the homes for women, and served as protectors for them. Freedman writes that:

> These women underwent intensive socialization into their roles as "true women." Combined with the restrictions on women which denied them access to the public sphere, this training gave American women an identity quite separate from men's.. . . . The

---

1. In this text, the terms "domestic violence" and "battered women" will be used virtually interchangeably. Neither term is sufficient for the crime, as convincingly argued by Ann Jones (1994). The term domestic violence removes the fact that this is a crime by men against women; the term neutralizes the clear and real gender disparity between victim and perpetrator. The term battered women, while recognizing the victims of these crimes, masks the constant nonphysical forms of violence (largely psychological), which are also employed by batterers and which also have a marked effect on their victims.

ideology of "true womanhood" was so deeply ingrained and so useful for preserving social stability in a time of flux that those few women who explicitly rejected its inequalities could find little support for their views. (1995, pp. 88–89)

The phrase "separate spheres" refers to this hypothesized division between the world of work and the world of home; one was seen as the place for women and the other as the place for men. (Although this division is now generally disputed, in large part it still serves to operationalize the treatment of domestic violence, and stereotypes based on this division are still largely functional in American society.) Middle-class white women participated in this system voluntarily (c.f. Helly and Reverby 1992; Kerber 1988; Rosaldo 1974; Rosenberg 1982; Sharistanian 1986, 1987). Rather than seeing it as a disadvantage, it was viewed by many as the opposite. In choosing this role, women traded economic power for "spiritual" power; this trade, like Esau's bargain, brought more regret than solace. As Rosenberg writes, "Women . . . were caught between two worlds—the Victorian world of domesticity with its restrictive view of femininity and the rapidly expanding commercial world of the late nineteenth and early twentieth centuries with its beckoning opportunities" (1982, p. xiv). Despite a dramatic shift in the number of women working in the formal marketplace in the last few decades, this public/private division has remained, as evidenced by the controversy over the teaching of sex education (a traditionally private sphere activity) in the public sphere of schooling. This same division hides domestic violence—it is seen as a "private" matter between a man and a woman.[2] Unfortunately, this invisibility of domestic violence also leads to the misconception that battering is limited to few, lower-class, or non-white women. None of these is true. In contrast, women from all walks of life are battered; the crime of domestic violence knows no boundaries of race, economics, or class. For example, "police in the mostly white, upper-class Washington D.C. suburb of Montgomery County, Maryland received the same amount of domestic disturbance calls as did Harlem, New York City, in the same period" (Refuge House 1992, p. 6-1).

The issues involved in domestic violence are emotionally and physically difficult as well as complex, and there are numerous texts that do justice to these intricacies (c.f. Bart and Moran 1993; Beaudry 1985; Berry 1996;

---

2. Approximately 4 percent of domestic violence is accounted for by men who are battered by women. It is also the case that women are battered by their lesbian partners and that men are battered by their gay male partners. However, the battering of women by men accounts for the vast majority of domestic violence. This text will refer to batterers as male and to victims as female for this reason.

Brown, Dubau, and McKeon 1997; Buzawa and Buzawa 1996; Crowell and Burgess 1996; Dutton 1995; Martin 1976; Mariani 1996; Schechter 1982; Statman 1995; Twerski 1996). In recognition of and deference to the body of literature that has been written by counselors, psychologists, and survivors on domestic violence, the purpose of this appendix is to provide a brief explanation of the dynamics of domestic violence and battered women's shelters to frame an exploration of the kinds of feminist education that are an integral part of the shelter movement. There are many topics that are not covered in this appendix, such as how to identify a potential batterer, how to plan for safety, and how to escape. Neither does this appendix dwell on counseling or educational techniques. These issues are interventions, and are presented with the narratives of shelter workers, volunteers, and domestic violence survivors. This appendix instead outlines domestic violence as an intricate, criminal, social phenomenon. This discussion will provide the background necessary to understand the function and nature of domestic violence shelters and their residents to inform the larger discussion of education as feminist movement that takes place within this movement and its shelters.

It is difficult to present domestic violence both briefly and thoroughly. As an issue it encompasses both personal trauma and societal failure. Battered women are at the center of a web of inadequate social structures and a set of mores that differentiates the violence they suffer at the hands of a partner from "real" violence. Real violence is punished, condemned, and sanctions are levied, while much domestic violence is ignored—or worse, reprimanded so lightly as to reinforce this view of triviality. There have been volumes written on domestic violence, which make these critical connections. The mission of this work, however, is different. Here domestic violence is painted in broad brush strokes in order to contextualize the education and learning that take place in its midst and its recovery, and as a modicum of understanding so that the silence forms a sound, and a name. This section accordingly has been phrased as a segment of volunteer training. Your entry as reader into this text is much like the entry of a volunteer into the world of women's silent pain.

Nowhere To Run To

Domestic violence is defined by its two constitutive terms: domestic and violence. *Domestic* violence takes place within relationships, most often between a man and a woman where the man is the aggressor and the woman is the target. These relationships can include marriages, common-law relationships, and dating relationships. This aspect of domestic violence—its placement within established relationships—is pivotal to understanding both the dynamics of the abuse and the difficulty of escape. To the eyes of the law, domestic violence is a different form of violence; the same acts that are perpetrated within these relationships would be prosecuted differently if they were perpetrated against strangers.

This is the second dimension: *violence*. This violence includes both physical and psychological abuse. In her notable 1979 work, Lenore Walker defines this violence as follows:

> A battered woman is a woman who is repeatedly subjected to any forceful physical or psychological behavior by a man in order to coerce her to do something he wants her to do without any concern for her rights. Battered women include wives or women in any form of intimate relationships with men. (p. xv)

The violence can take place over weeks, years, or decades. The key to domestic violence, as this appendix will explore, is that it is not isolated incidences of violence. Instead it represents a clear pattern that cycles and repeats over time. As defined by the Tallahassee Refuge House:

> Battering is a pattern of behavior that seeks to establish power and control over another person through fear and intimidation. It often includes the threat or use of violence. Battering happens when batterers believe they are entitled to control their partners. They believe that the violence is acceptable and will produce the desired results. Not all battering is physical. Battering involves emotional abuse, economic abuse, sexual abuse, threats to and about children, using "male privilege," intimidation, isolation, and other behaviors used to induce fear and establish power. Battering escalates. It may begin with name-calling or punching a wall or kicking a pet. Next steps may be pushing, slapping, pinching; then punching, kicking, biting, tripping, throwing, or restraining. It often includes sexual assault. It may lead to choking, the breaking of bones, or other life-threatening incidents. (p. 6–1)

The existence of this cycle is recognizable across women's experiences, and the systematic nature of this violence sets it apart from other forms of violence, often performed out of passion, "in the heat of the moment."

It is critical to note that the term *domestic violence* is a legal one. It does not arise from battered women themselves, who refer to themselves as "victims," "survivors," or "battered women." The term *domestic violence* is clinical; it removes the individual from the act. Neither "domestic violence" nor "battered women" subsumes the myriad of issues involved in this form of injury to women. Domestic violence removes the fact that *women* are battered by *men*. Referring to the act as physical battering removes the psychological and emotional dimensions of the violence.[3] While neither term is adequate, they will be used interchangeably within this work as they often are by the shelter movement, with the recognition and caveat that neither represents the entirety of the issue.

Faces of Victims: Faces of Friends

The raw numbers which describe incidents of domestic violence in a year do not speak to issues of race, class, or socioeconomic status. They fail to reveal domestic violence as a crime that crosses all of these barriers. As one volunteer manual states: There is no "typical battered personality. The risk factor is often being born female." Battered women are married or dating; have children or are childless; are employed or are homemakers. They are white, black, Chicana, Latina, Asian, Indian, and all other races and ethnicities. They are Jewish, Christian, and atheist. They are multiply lingual and multiply abled. In fact, their shared experience as battered women is the only link between these disparate groups:

> Although there is no profile of the woman who will be battered, there is a well-documented syndrome of what happens once the battering starts. Battered women experience shame, embarrassment, isolation, repression of feelings, and may be prevented by control and fear from planning or acting on their own behalf. Women may not leave battering immediately because they realistically fear that the batterer will become more violent if they attempt to leave, there are few supports to their leaving, they know the difficulties of single parenting in reduced financial circumstances, [and] there is a mix of good times-love-hope along with manipulation-intimidation-fear. (Refuge House 1992, p. 6-9)

Women of all races and economic circumstances are battered. Women who are poor—whether because of economic abuse or a lack of household resources—are equally likely to be battered but are more likely to seek and to need shelter and resources.

Faces of Control: Faces of Men

Men who batter similarly come from all socioeconomic backgrounds, races, religions, and circumstances. Some batterers come from a family history of violence; others do not. Just as there is no typical battered woman, there is

---

3. For an informative discussion of this issue of naming, see Jones op cit.

no typical batterer that could be recognized either as a stranger on the street or in the beginning of a relationship. There are, however, common themes among batterers, some of which further complicate their portrait. For example, most batterers are only violent with their female partners. Within the shelter movement, this is referred to as the Jekyll-Hyde effect; batterers appear to be two different people—the man who batters his wife and the affable, smiling colleague and friend to others. This effectively contributes to the silencing that becomes part of domestic violence relationships: it is often too late when friends and relatives discover black eyes and bruises. Friends and family, who often know and see the positive aspects of the batterer, refuse to believe the victim and often blame the victim (or tell her she's crazy) rather than intervening on her behalf.

It is terrifying to think that violent men are unrecognizable to women beginning relationships and that these men (who often are not violent in the beginning) become violent with their partners without warning. To some extent this is true: many women do not experience violence, for example, until they are pregnant. However, there are some warning signs or characteristics of potentially abusive partners, including: intense jealousy, experiences of violence during childhood, hatred of mother, quick temper, substance abuse, rigid role expectations, controlling behaviors, displaced aggression, or aggression directed at objects. According to the National Coalition Against Domestic Violence, these signs are recognizable in family violence.

Although there is no typical personality pattern, there are common characteristics among abusers. As Refuge House relates:

> A major characteristic of assailants in domestic violence cases is their capacity for self-deception and the deception of others. . . . Their primary, if not exclusive, emotional investment is with a conjugal partner, and the assailant experiences an intense desire to control this individual. . . . The assailant is likely to become most violent if the partner threatens or attempts to leave. Battering can be seen as an extreme expression of the belief in male dominance over women. To understand why men choose to batter, it is important to look at what they get out of using violence. Men use physical force to maintain power and control over their relationships with their female partners. They have learned that violence works to achieve this end. (1992, pp. 7-1–7-2)

Men who batter are not physically or psychologically ill; battering is a learned behavior and it is a choice.

I'm Sorry . . . Forgive Me . . .

Relationships do not usually *begin* with violence. If, for example, a woman went on a first date with a man who became abusive and hit her, that date would most likely be their last. Violence begins slowly and not always physically. The movie *What's Love Got To Do With It*, which relates the life and abusive relationship of Ike and Tina Turner, is quite accurate in this regard. The violence begins slowly: Ike whisks Tina out of the hospital (where she is being treated for extreme exhaustion and anemia) against the doctor's orders—but in order to marry her. "How is this violent?", one might ask. It is violent because Ike risks Tina's health to get his own way—to retain and reinforce his control over her. He then begins putting her down in front of other group members and her family, telling her that he alone is responsible for her success. Throughout the movie, it becomes evident that he is employing another tactic frequently used by abusers; Ike also controls all of Tina's money. It is only later that Ike physically abuses her, and these two factors are seen in sharp focus when Tina, battered and bloody, stumbles to a Ramada Inn escaping from Ike and reveals that while she is Tina Turner, the recording star, she has only "36 cents and a Mobil card."

Violence and abuse in relationships begin in ways that seem relatively innocuous and are actually reinforced in part by society. While each of these factors, taken apart, does not equal a violent relationship, the combination of factors can point to violence. Each of these factors may or may not be present in any given relationship. The overarching effect of a combination of these factors is that of control over another human being—in the case of domestic violence, of a man over his female partner.[4] The following sections describe isolation, economics, threats and coercion, intimidation, emotional abuse, minimizing and blaming, using children and male privilege as the tools, pressures, and rationales used to maintain an abusive relationship. The battered woman who tries to escape, like the slave, is venturing into dangerous territory where few are on her side. The battered woman who escapes is an émigré in her own country, often bereft of family and friends.

Isolation

Even the term *isolation* brings to mind prisoners, hostages, or desert islands. These images are at once correct and unrecognizable in the beginning of a

---

4. Although there are instances of women battering men, and of same-sex partner batterings, 96 percent of all victims of domestic violence are women with male abusers. Therefore this text makes no attempt to utilize gender-balanced language. It is a grim reality of domestic violence that its victims are female and its perpetuators male.

violent relationship. Isolation can begin as jealousy, where a man may tell his partner that he wants her to spend all of her time with him (and not her family or friends). In the U.S. culture of social dyad relationships where the romantic relationship takes precedence over friendships (cf. Holland and Eisenhart 1990) this seems normal, even touching, and appropriate for a new relationship. Jealousy in a violent relationship, however, is a manifestation of both isolation—the removal of resources available to women through family and friends—and of the overarching power and control that is fundamental to domestic violence. In the case of the battered woman, jealousy and controlling behaviors result in her isolation from a support network of people who might either resist his actions or help her.

Isolation also moves beyond mere jealousy in this case. For some women, isolation in their relationships results in control over what she does, who she sees, what she reads, or where she goes. In essence, isolation can imply a total removal of resources and information that are critical to a woman's survival. Consider the example of a man who, when friends call for his wife, takes messages and then destroys them so that the wife believes no one has called. The friends feel slighted (she doesn't return calls) and the wife feels lonely or ignored by her friends (who aren't calling). For as long as the husband continues to intercept these messages, these beliefs are perpetuated. In time, he does not need to intercept: calls are neither made nor received because he has created a rift in the relationship. These means of isolation can be very subtle, as in this case, or quite direct, as when a male forbids his partner to see family or friends. The result is the same: if a woman decides to seek help, she has fewer sources from whom to seek it. There are fewer witnesses to black eyes and unexplainable bruises, and there is a loss of friends to whom a woman can turn.

Economics

Economic abuse, which results in a woman having few resources of her own with which to seek help, also is a common factor in domestic violence. There are two ways in which this is generally structured. In the first, the man controls his partner's income by maintaining control over the joint checking account or by taking her paycheck and giving her a limited amount of money for household expenditures for which she must account. This is reinforced by societal stereotypes about men being in control of the household as well as the common stereotype that men are better with figures. As the man, in charge of "his" household, batterers often feel they have the right to control all aspects of the household income (Ike Turner is again an example). The second way in which economics are logistically structured is where a man refuses to allow his partner to work. In extreme cases he may lock her inside the house to which only he has the key, take the only vehicle, and remove the telephone so that she literally has no escape. In other cases, the man may show up and make unpleasant scenes at her place of employment, either costing her the job or shaming her into quitting. Once the job is lost, however, this often becomes a topic for additional emotional abuse—"You weren't good enough"; "They would have fired you."

The results of economic abuse are similar to those of isolation: it limits a woman's options to find help. Women who consider leaving their abusive partners must be able to support themselves as well as any dependent children. It is no accident that divorced women suffer a dramatic loss in their real incomes while divorced men experience a clear gain. Women who have been out of the job market for a significant period of time may lack skills to make them employable and may be unequipped to look for a job. Women who flee also need short-term resources for housing, food, and other expenses while they search for employment (as well as dealing with the court system, child protective services, and the emotional trauma of their experiences).

Threats and Coercion

Threats play on many fears. The most obvious threat is to do bodily harm to a woman or to her children. Women in violent relationships learn to believe these threats as they become reality. Threats of physical harm are also a form of psychological violence, used to control a woman's actions as she attempts to escape or mitigate the violence. Other threats are often an even more powerful form of control. Men threaten, for example, to call Child Protective Services and report that a woman has been abusing her children (when in reality it is the man who has inflicted the violence). In this threat, the implicit fear of not being believed innocent is combined with the fear of losing one's children. In some states, if a parent is aware of but does not report child abuse, the innocent parent is also considered guilty for not reporting; if a woman does report child abuse, the man again threatens to (and often does) blame the woman as responsible for the violence against the children. The man may also threaten to leave the woman, particularly if he is the sole economic provider, and may combine this threat with constant emotional abuse about her worthlessness ("You'll never make it without me."). If she attempts to leave, he may threaten to commit suicide, playing on her sympathies. If she attempts to call the police, he may threaten to tell them that the violent episode was her fault, or that they were both to blame; in this case, they may both be arrested and children may be taken into protective custody.

Intimidation

Intimidation follows closely on the use of coercion and threats. Intimidation is one way of reminding a woman inside or outside the home that violence is a constant reality. Women who have been battered in long-term relationships often report that their male partners could just speak a simple phrase, such as "I'll get you" and that they would be terrified, knowing what he meant. Intimidation can also involve violence directed at something other than the woman. He may destroy her personal property, particularly emotionally laden items such as photographs. This is intimidating because it is a show of strength—the clear message is "you could be next." He may kill or abuse her pets. Consider the case of a woman pilot who left to fight in the Gulf War. When she returned from her assignment, her pets had all disappeared; they had been "given away" by her husband because they were "too much trouble." Men who intimidate do so by showing how far they are willing to go, by reminding women of the constant possibility of violence, and occasionally by carrying weapons or talking about ways in which they intend to hurt, torture, or kill the woman. In the Academy Award–winning documentary *Defending Our Lives*, one story is related about a woman whose husband tells her, again and again, that he is going to kill her. He keeps her chained behind the house, depriving her of regular food and water. He tells her that he will drown her, and she watches him have a human-size tank built in the front yard. She had every reason to believe would carry out his threat and kill her, and in fact she kills him on the very day that she believes she is to die.

Emotional Abuse

Many women, according to Lenore Walker, view their own experience of emotional abuse as worse than the physical abuse. Emotional abuse plays on a woman's fears and insecurities. It may begin with questioning her abilities—to cook, to clean the house, to perform other "women's work"; to perform at her job; or to be a good parent. It may also be directed at her self-image; for example, an abuser may tell his partner that she is ugly, fat, and unlovable—and that without him she would be absolutely alone. An abuser may put his partner down with these kinds of verbal slams in front of others—co-workers, family, and friends, and he may do so in such a way that the abuse is only evident as an underlying tone. As this type of abuse progresses, the abuser may humiliate his partner in front of others, make her think that she is crazy, or making her feel guilty about her less-than-perfect actions. This form of abuse often creates the mindset in the victim that she can control the abuse—by being a better homemaker, wife, or mother; by losing weight or changing her appearance; or by any act that she performs. The reality is, however, the abuse is not within her control and her actions are not the catalyst for the abuse.

Minimizing and Blaming

This tactic utilized by abusers also contributes to the mindset that the abuse is either the woman's fault or not serious. In many cases, the abuser tells the victim that she has "no sense of humor" or that "it's only a bruise." This is different from the cycle of violence where the abuser may apologize for his actions and promise that they will never be repeated. One example of minimizing was directed at me. I was stalked by a dating partner who in one evening broke into my car, attempted to break into my home, and terrorized me through an entire night while I lay in the dark, virtually petrified with fear and unable to summon the courage to cross in front of the windows to reach a phone and call for help. In the morning, he told me to laugh about the incident and offered to take me to breakfast. When I refused (and called the police) he told me—and the police, and his friends—that he had "only been joking" and that "no one would care about what happens to a secretary" (which I was at the time). To this, he added the threat that his well-connected father would ensure that he served no jail time.

Similar to minimizing is blaming a victim for the acts committed against her. To blame the victim (a tactic employed by both abusers and bystanders) is to tell her that the abuse is her fault, and that if she had performed better it would have been avoided. Del Martin quotes the following passage from a letter from a battered wife: "I have learned also that the doctors, the police, the clergy, and my friends will excuse my husband for distorting my face, but won't forgive me for looking bruised and broken" (1995, p. 48).

Common forms of blame concern the same topics used in emotional abuse—a woman's ability to care for her home, her children, and her appearance. Domestic violence is, in fact, not the woman's fault and there is little she can do to contain it for long. If dinner is precisely on time, the abuser will find fault with her cooking. If the cooking is excellent, the abuser will disparage the presentation, the cleanliness of the kitchen, or the condition of the children's clothing. It is clear from these descriptions that several forms of this abuse follow from the batterers' characteristic acceptance of and belief in rigid sex-role stereotypes in which women are responsible for maintaining a perfect home and children without assistance. Battered women are often both frantic to please their abuser—to lessen the threat of immediate violence—and accepting of their partner's judgment of them as bad mothers, wives, or homemakers. As Refuge House again writes:

> The most powerful enticement for the victims to blame themselves is the fantasy that, if they provoked or elicited the beating, then they can control or eliminate the assault simply by being "good." Ironically, though the shift of responsibility may meet some immediate desires for reassurance of both assailant and victim, this shift enhances the likelihood of further assaults. . . . In actual fact, the assaults are a product of the assailant's personality structure, and have little relationship to external events such as victim behavior. (p. 7-2)

Another form of minimization and blaming is to deny that the abuse ever happened. An assailant may tell his partner that he never hit her, that she "doesn't remember" walking into the door, or falling down the stairs. This form of minimization dovetails with emotional abuse, or making a woman feel (and fear) that she is "going crazy." An analogy can easily be drawn to Hitchcock's famous film *Gaslight*, which features a man's attempt to convince his wife that she (rather than having discovered him in what appears to be criminal activity) instead is insane.

Using Children

Children often are pawns in violent relationships. The abuser may either threaten to hurt them or actually do so. He may also threaten to take them away or to report that she is abusing them (when in actuality he is their abuser as well as the abuser of his partner). If a woman leaves with her children, the abuser may threaten to sue her for primary custody and then deny her visitation. Alternately, he may threaten to leave with the children so that she will never see them again. Children factor into nearly every one of the other tactics, whether as a source for guilt (she is a bad mother, or it is her fault that they are exposed to so much violence); economic abuse (when she considers that she cannot support them and herself without his income); or blaming (when he teaches the children that the abuse is their mother's "fault").

When women succeed in leaving, the courts do often award joint custody, and the abuser can and often does use the opportunity of visitation to further his harassment or sends messages via the children that their mother is bad, shouldn't be respected, or that he will hurt her. Children are also used as pawns to further the violence against their mother by being taught that the father is correct in "disciplining" his wife and that she is not to be listened to, trusted, or believed.

Male Privilege

Male privilege is fundamental to violent relationships. As a tactic, abusers may treat their partners like servants, demanding services both sexual and menial. However, this is even more definitively a belief that is foundational to the violent relationship. Reinforced by and reinforcing his belief in women's roles is the abuser's belief in himself as the primary decision maker. As the one in control, the abuser sees it as his fundamental "right" to abuse his partner, to utilize these tactics, and to not be sanctioned for his actions. Above all other tactics, this one is reinforced most directly by the societal belief in gender roles and in the private world where a husband can maintain absolute control.

As these tactics have illustrated, violence and violent acts are both varied in type and intensity; they exist along a continuum, both physical and psychological. Each type of violence is harmful; while psychological abuse does not often send women to the emergency room, it works in tandem with, or sets the stage for, other forms of violence and limits a woman's means of escape. The following diagram illustrates the continuum.

PHYSICAL ABUSE CONTINUUM

Conventional Violence
(Accepted in child rearing by 87–94% of all families)

- Ignoring or not meeting needs of dependent
- Pinch/Squeeze
- Push-Shove-Restrain
- Jerk-Pull-Shake
- Slap-Bite-Pull hair
- Shake, leaving bruises
- Hit-Punch-Kick

Battering/Victimization:
(Men do this to women more often and with more serious injuries)

- Choke-Throw objects
- Repeated use of previous items*
- Targeted hitting*
- Restraining & Hitting, Punching*
- Medical Treatment Needed*
- Lacerations that require stitches*
- Throwing victim*
- Miscarriage or forced abortion*
- Use of objects as weapons
    (household weapons)*
- Denial of medical treatment*
- Use of weapons
    (guns/knives/poison)*
- Disabling or disfiguring injuries*
- Homicide*

---

* These provide evidence that the man is not out of control when he batters. He is using violence to control and punish the woman. Emotional/psychological and sexual abuse may occur in conjunction with physical battering at any stage. These kinds of abuse also escalate in severity.

Even the milder forms of violence on this continuum, however, seem to be enough to cause a woman to try to escape from the situation. Given this variety of tactics and the clear violence, both emotional and physical, it is clear that there is a larger pattern operating that traps women in these relationships. Within the domestic relationship, the pattern is one of power and control.

Out of Control

The tactics described earlier fall on what is known as the power and control wheel. The symbol of a wheel represents the cycles and interactions of all of these forms of violent actions against women. Power and control are written at the center of the wheel because they are the central concepts around

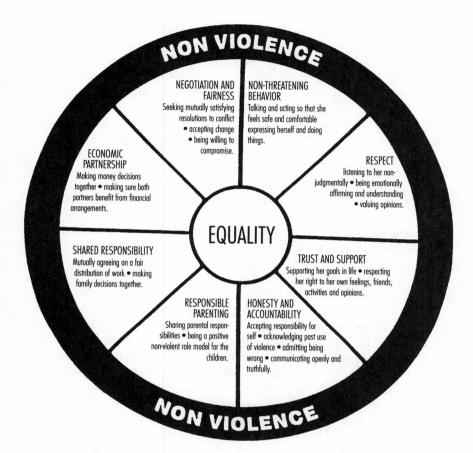

which the violent acts are arrayed. Acts that otherwise seem to make no sense become clear when considered through this lens. For example, if battering were a woman's fault, or if she were a "bad" wife and mother, it would seem self-evident that if she left her partner he would be grateful. Instead, when a woman tries to leave she is in the most danger. Domestic violence is a means by which a man maintains (often total) control over a woman. One tactic in domestic violence counseling[5] is to present the opposing wheel, which is based around equality. The previous diagrams present both wheels.

---

5. Women who are battered are not mentally ill and do not require psychological intervention in most cases. However, their experiences need to be validated and they often lack models of "normal" relationships because of these experiences.

However, even given the series of physical and psychological forms of violence perpetrated in domestic violence, including the tactics by which women are systematically denied their rights and resources, domestic violence is still hard to understand. One common question is why women stay. The question itself is implicated in blaming the victim; after all, it would make more sense to ask why men are abusive. But in a positive light, the question represents concern for the victim. If a woman is suffering from these forms of abuse, particularly in the beginning of the cycle where the violence may occur less often or with less drastic consequences, what prevents her from leaving?

As an earlier section mentioned, violence does not start immediately. A further revelation is that it is also not constant. Lenore Walker developed the cycle of violence to explain the three-stage sequence often repeated in abusive relationships. In the first phase, tension builds. Women often describe this as "walking on eggshells" and relate that it is during this phase where they make the most efforts to please their partners—by keeping the children quiet, making the house immaculate, or other behaviors to "keep a low profile." No matter what extreme efforts she makes, however, the next phase in the cycle is an acute battering incident. While this is the most violent phase, sometimes involving severe physical injuries, it is also the shortest phase, and is followed by what is perhaps the most powerful stage in the cycle. The third phase is called the "honeymoon" phase, during which the abuser acts ashamed and apologetic. It is during this stage where he may act like "the man I married," bringing gifts, giving compliments, buying dinner, and perhaps promising to get counseling. Understanding this cycle makes it easier to understand why a woman might choose to stay with her partner—the man she loves and has chosen to be with—and might believe him when he promises that "it will never happen again" and that he will seek help. The following diagram illustrates the interaction as an ongoing cycle. These phases initially can be quite long, with up to six months between phases. However, in most battered women's experience, the cycle spins faster, with more acute injuries and less honeymoon; sometimes the honeymoon disappears altogether. (See Cycle of Violence diagram.)

Are You Ready, My Sister?

This phrase from a slave song, originating in the American slavery experience, recognizes the fact that a victim must be ready to escape. She cannot be merely removed forcibly from her situation. Any reader familiar with trauma will recognize that victims and survivors do not exist in a constant state of fear, nor do they exist in a constant state of hope, struggle, empowerment, or helplessness. Some women who come to shelter are depressed,

Cycle of Violence

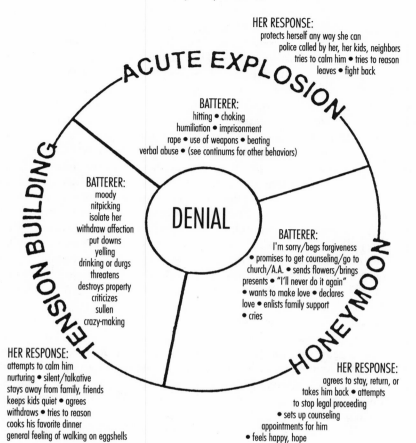

HER RESPONSE:
protects herself any way she can
police called by her, her kids, neighbors
tries to calm him • tries to reason
leaves • fight back

ACUTE EXPLOSION

BATTERER:
hitting • choking
humiliation • imprisonment
rape • use of weapons • beating
verbal abuse • (see continuums for other behaviors)

TENSION BUILDING

BATTERER:
moody
nitpicking
isolate her
withdraw affection
put downs
yelling
drinking or durgs
threatens
destroys property
criticizes
sullen
crazy-making

DENIAL

BATTERER:
I'm sorry/begs forgiveness
• promises to get counseling/go to
church/A.A. • sends flowers/brings
presents • "I'll never do it again"
• wants to make love • declares
love • enlists family support
• cries

HONEYMOON

HER RESPONSE:
attempts to calm him
nurturing • silent/talkative
stays away from family, friends
keeps kids quiet • agrees
withdraws • tries to reason
cooks his favorite dinner
general feeling of walking on eggshells

HER RESPONSE:
agrees to stay, return, or
takes him back • attempts
to stop legal proceeding
• sets up counseling
appointments for him
• feels happy, hope

How denial works in each stage of the cycle to keep the cycle going.
(Only by breaking through this denial can the cycle be broken.)

1. TENSION BUILDING
She denies it's happening, excuses it as some outside stress (work, etc.); blames herself for his behavior, denies that the abuse will worsen. He denies by blaming the tension on her, work, the traffic, anything: by getting drunk, denies responsibility for his actions.

2. EXPLOSION
She denies her injuries, only minor ("I bruise easily"), didn't require police or medical help; blames it on drinking ("He didn't know what he was doing."); does not label it rape because it was her husband.
He blames it on her, stress, etc. ("She had it coming.")

3. HONEYMOON
She minimizes injuries ("It could have been worse."); believes this is the way it will stay, the man of her dreams, believes his promises.
He also believes it won't happen again.

often sleeping around the clock or manifesting odd or irregular eating or sleeping habits. Other women nurture new women coming to the house, watching their children and baking sweets for the house. Some women leave shelter to return to their abusers; others leave their families, cities, and even states in a conclusive effort of finality. The existence of these multiple reactions is confusing to those trying to understand the battered woman's experience. In reality, this experience, while not singular or simple, does follow a recognizable pattern just as their experiences of violence follow a pattern that once known becomes obvious. However, these differing reactions also feed into a set of myths about battering and battered women.

Women who are battered may deny that they are being battered; this is the stereotypical image of a woman telling her friend that she "walked into a wall" rather than admit that her black eye or broken arm is attributable to violence within her home. Ironically, this denial often keeps women from seeking assistance in the early stages of abuse and contributes to their own entrapment. Women may then blame themselves, as discussed earlier—for being an imperfect wife, mother, homemaker, or sexual partner. This self-blame also contributes to whether or not a woman seeks assistance; a woman who blames herself and continues to do so will exhaust all options for "improving" herself before moving into the next stage, which is where a woman does seek help.

These stages are not developmental in the Piagetian or Ericksonian sense of the term; rather than fixed periods, these stages can extend for years and there is no guarantee that a woman will either go through all of them or that she will do so in the proscribed order or indeed that she will survive to the end of the series. A woman may remain in the denial or self-blame stages for an indeterminate amount of time; often there is an incident that prompts her into the next stage, seeking help. This incident in many women's experience is when the violence extends to their children and they fear not only for themselves but for the rest of their families. I answered many hotline calls from women who describe this experience as "something snapped and I had to get out." This is the stage where women who are able to do so seek help and some receive it. Sometimes this means entering shelter, which is not a casual choice for either women or shelters. Entering shelter often means leaving behind most or all personal belongings, moving from a private residence to a group living situation, and losing face because of their "inability" to survive without assistance. Shelters similarly face a difficult decision with each admittance. Most cities have few shelters (if any) and beds are extremely limited. In Washington, D.C., the nation's capital and a city of millions, there are two shelters: one with 21 beds and the other with 24. In Tallahassee, Florida, the state's capital, the shelter serves seven counties with 24 beds. Women are turned away because shelters are full, or because they have other options (sometimes unsafe housing or reluctant family members). Many shelters only take women from out of their cachement area in dire emergencies (and like the Underground Railroad, women do flee from shelter to shelter to leave their home states and struggle for new, safer lives elsewhere) so that there are available spaces for local women needing assistance.

In the midst of this difficult decision to seek help and sometimes to leave, women are often ambivalent, questioning their decision. Living in shelter promotes this thinking. Imagine the scenario just described—a woman has left her home, her belongings, and her privacy and is now in shelter with her children. Her children are acting out because they are also frightened and uncomfortable and perhaps because they have been taught not to respect their mother. Perhaps her children are also saying that they miss their "daddy." The woman has fled her abuser but still loves him. She may be pressured from family or friends who lack understanding of the problem to return, and may be further faced with financial difficulties of finding housing, employment, or pursuing child support and custody. These are the grim realities that women confront, and it is not difficult to recognize how ambivalence can figure into this picture with regularity.

Women who are ambivalent about terminating their relationship may pursue counseling as an option to try to change the relationship itself. Some women seek court-ordered counseling for their partners in the hope that these men will change. Other women go in and out of their relationships, returning to shelters or other residences between periods of reconciliation. Sometimes women in shelter (who agree not to see their partners during the period of time that they are in residence) secretly meet their abusers and reconcile. These reconciliations can result in living without violence, for some period of time. It is unclear what the recidivism rate is among men who have sought or have attended counseling, or among "reformed" batterers in general. This is the fifth stage: living without violence. Not all battered women reach this stage, whether they are unable to escape permanently from their partners or whether they choose, for whatever reason, to remain in a violent relationship. Some women enter multiple violent relationships; having successfully terminated one, they find themselves with a second abusive partner. Success in this stage can be defined either as remaining in the relationship (nonviolently) or as ending the relationship and at that point living free from violence.

Discussing the stages of a battered woman's experience, however generally, still tends to point the finger at psychological or individual difficulties rather than at a larger social structure engendering and lending both tacit and overt support to the violence perpetrated against women in their own homes. Earlier in this appendix, the historical division of private and public spheres was discussed as a social rather than individual phenomenon. Similarly, the existence of domestic violence within this private sphere is also a social phenomenon. The pattern that exists across women and across batterers points to a problem well beyond the reach of personal dysfunction and individual failure. In fact, there are recognizable elements of social support of these violent relationships throughout the governance structures of the United States, both locally and in states as well as nationally. The well-recognized elements of racism, sexism, and homophobia contribute to this environment in which women's struggles are met with hostile silence. Ironically, it is when women are struggling to escape that they meet with the most danger—like the escaped slave on the Underground Railway. Battering, like slavery, causes discomfort when it breaks the barriers of its secrecy and silence.

I Wish I Were a Boy

The previous pages have sketched the kinds of abuse that occur within the context of domestic violence in terms of both the violent experiences and tactics employed to gain and keep power and control. The overarching concepts of power and control, and in particular power and control over women, are repeating themes throughout history and have been detailed by a number of feminist scholars (c.f. Bunch and Pollack 1983; Evans 1979; Firestone 1972; hooks 1984; Jaggar 1983; Kahn 1995; Morris and Mueller 1992). Consider the pervasive power of expectations, as revealed by social theorists such as Foucault (particularly with regard to labeling) and Goffman (in terms of social interaction). Although many contemporary women scoff at so-called "old fashioned" notions of women's role and appropriate, feminine behaviors, these ideas are pervasive at fundamental levels. Susan Faludi documents the number of female stereotypes that are still used in today's media—the stereotypes that tell women not to rebel or they will be considered "bitches," "whores," or worse—"lesbians" or "spinsters." The title of Schur's book states this clearly: *Labeling Women Deviant: Gender, Stigma, and Social Control.* Men (particularly white, middle-class men) have clear positions of advantage in American society, and this advantage extends into the maintenance of rigid sex roles for women—including obedience and subservience to men, including those who batter.

Sexism also leads to differential treatment of crimes against women in the legal and judicial systems. In the case of crimes against women, the system's traditional response has been one of nonintervention and of blaming the victim (as in the well-documented case of rape trials). Crimes against women are considered less serious than those against men—and crimes against women committed by their partners are hardly considered crimes at all. Women are victimized by social norms and expectations, brutalized by their partners, and then battered again by the systems they face when trying to escape.

Racism and homophobia also affect the response of the general public as well as law enforcement agencies and officers to domestic violence. A common myth is that domestic violence only takes place in racially nonwhite neighborhoods. Homophobia plays into sex-role stereotypes, as women are threatened with being negatively viewed as lesbian for either leaving a relationship or for working against domestic violence. Further, it is often assumed that only heterosexual women are battered—and that all women are heterosexual (straight). As a point of fact, the vast majority of battering relationships involve a male aggressor and a female victim; however, domestic violence is not limited to this classic relationship formation. This book is dedicated to a lesbian battered and then killed by her [female] partner.

In many ways, domestic violence, like slavery, is a web of interlocking experiences and beliefs. To trace one pattern, rigid sex role stereotypes of women as unfit for the labor market—but as the ideal wife and mother—leads into women's dependence on men economically as well as the potential for self-blame when failing to meet unrealistic expectations. Both of these then limit independence and the ability to gather resources (emotional and financial) for escape. Alternately, consider the social myth of "staying together for the sake of the children" and its implications for battered women.

These are social factors that extend into individual women's lives but follow a sociological pattern of hierarchy and control. In other words, the homes of battered women often represent a microcosm of the larger social universe, where the same roles play out. In some homes, the social world plays out in the double working world of women, or Arlie Hochschild's "second shift" (see also Blumberg 1991). In other homes the differential power and control of men is taken to a more dramatic, and more violent, extreme. Nonetheless, each represents a social dynamic rather than an individual dilemma; while individual men commit the crime of battering, they are following a socially established and reinforced (but not inevitable) pattern. Aafke Kemter writes that issues of power and equality are changing but not diminishing:

> As men's formal and institutionalized power decreases in Western societies, informal and not necessarily institutionalized ways of sustaining and reproducing power inequality between women and men are becoming more visible. (1989, p. 187)

These new ways of viewing power hold great promise for educational and feminist revolution in terms of re-viewing learning, schooling, education, and the ways in which women's politicized lives intersect with these activities. The focus of sociological educational work has been changing over the past decade—first, from a static view of the system as immutable to hegemonic and constantly constructed; and now, to an interest in the actors and agency rather than the terminal act of oppression. Dorothy Holland and Margaret Eisenhart predicted that:

> Although the importance of regimes of power and privilege has certainly not been erased from the theoretical picture, the spotlight has swung away from the means by which the powerful maintain hegemony. More recently emphasized, both in theory and in research, are the cultural productions of the less powerful. (1990, p. 41)

Battered women in American society constitute part of the "less powerful." The truth in Holland and Eisenhart's prediction is seen in the work of Kathleen Casey (1993), Michelle Fine (1992), Mara Sapon-Shevin (1994), Lois Weis (1993), and others who write of women's lives, adolescent's lives, black lives, and whose focus is on these lives as they resist and construct new ways of being and change. This study is part of a long and critical tradition of working with women to inform theory and to create understanding and change.

Appendix B

Domestic Violence Timeline, with Key Slavery-Related Dates

ca. 1820   Harriet Tubman born

ca. 1849   Harriet Tubman escapes and begins leading slaves to freedom along the Underground Railroad.

             Colonial American women form networks to assist women in fleeing from abusive husbands.

1865   Thirteenth Amendment to the U.S. Constitution is passed and ratified, emancipating the slaves.

1964   First women's shelter formed.

1971   Chiswick Women's Aid, the first recognized shelter, opens in England.

1972   Women's Advocates in St. Paul, Minnesota, start the first hotline for battered women. Women's Advocates and Haven House in Pasadena, California, establish the first recognized shelter for battered women in the United States.

1974   Erin Prizzley publishes *Scream Quietly or the Neighbors Will Hear* in England, the first book about domestic violence from the battered woman's perspective.

1975   The Jacksonville Women's Movement purchases Hubbard House, the first emergency shelter specifically for battered women in the Southeast and thirteenth in the nation.

1976   NOW announces the formation of a task force to examine the problem of battering. It demands research into the problem and funding for shelters.

Del Martin publishes *Battered Wives*, which originates the idea of a "cycle of violence."

Nebraska becomes the first state to abolish the marital rape exemption.

Pennsylvania establishes the first state coalition against domestic violence. It also becomes the first state to create a statue providing for orders of protection for victims of domestic violence.

1977   Oregon becomes the first state to enact legislation mandating arrest in domestic violence cases.

1978   National Coalition Against Domestic Violence formed.

Minnesota becomes the first state to allow probable cause (warrantless arrest in cases of domestic assault, regardless of whether a protection order has been issued against the offender).

1979   Refuge House opens in Tallahassee, Florida.

My Sister's Place opens in Washington, D.C.

Office of Domestic Violence is established in U.S. Department of Health and Human Services but is closed in 1981.

First congressional hearings on the issue of domestic violence are held.

1983   A Police Foundation study in Minneapolis, funded by the National Institute of Justice, finds arrest more effective than two nonarrest alternatives in reducing the likelihood of repeat violence. The study findings are widely publicized and provide the impetus for many police departments to establish pro-arrest policies in cases of domestic violence.

1984   U.S. Attorney General establishes Task Force on Family Violence to examine scope and nature of problem. Nearly 300 witnesses provide testimony at public hearings in six cities. The final report offers recommendations for action in many areas, including the criminal justice response, prevention and awareness, education and training, and data collection and reporting. Passage of the Family Violence Prevention and Services Act due to grassroots lobbying efforts; earmarks federal funding for programs serving victims of domestic violence.

Florida becomes the first state to enact legislation mandating consideration of spouse abuse in child custody determinations.

1985   *Thurman* v. *Torrington* is the first case in federal court in which a batttered woman sues a city for police fraud to protect her husband's violence. Tracy Thurman, who remains scarred and partially paralyzed from stab wounds inflicted by her husband, wins a $2 million judgment against the city. The suit leads to Connecticut's passage of its mandatory arrest law.

U.S. Surgeon General issues a report identifying domestic violence as a major health problem.

1987   National Clearinghouse for the Defense of Battered Women opens within the ACLU.

NCADV establishes first toll-free hotline for battered women.

1988   *State* v. *Ciskie* is the first case to allow the use of expert testimony to establish the mental state of an adult rape victim. The testimony is used to show why a victim of repeated physical and sexual assault by her intimate partner would not immediately call the police or take action. The jury convicts the defendant of four counts of rape.

1990   The Clothesline Project begins in Cape Cod, Massachusetts.

1991   First woman is granted clemency under the battered women's syndrome; the National Clearinghouse estimates that 39 women have been granted clemency, 1991–1998.

1993   *Defending Our Lives*, which documents the stories of battered women, wins an Academy Award for best short documentary.

1994   Violence Against Women Act passed as part of 1994 Crime Bill, forming the Violence Against Women Office in the U.S. Department of Justice.

1995   Violence Against Women Office opens.

1995	Trial of O.J. Simpson for the murder of his estranged wife, Nicole Brown Simpson, and her friend, Ronald Goldman.
1996	Acquittal of O.J. Simpson.
1996	Civil trial of O.J. Simpson for the murders of Ronald Goldman and Nicole Brown Simpson.
1998	O.J. Simpson convicted in civil court.
1999	Legal challenge against the constitutionality of VAWA.

Adapted from: Schechter, 1992; Refuge House, 1992; and various other sources.

Appendix C

Teaching and Learning with Adults

The differences between andragogy and pedagogy were first delineated by Malcolm Knowles, who defines andragogy as "the art and science of helping adults learn" (1970). According to Davenport and Davenport (1985),

> Knowles' theory was based upon four assumptions which distinguished adult learning from childhood learning: (1) as a person matures the self-concept moves from dependency toward self-direction; (2) maturity brings an accumulating reservoir of experience that becomes an increasing resource for learning; (3) as the person matures, readiness to learn is increasingly oriented towards the person's social roles; and (4) as the person matures the orientation towards learning becomes less subject-centered and increasingly problem-centered. (p. 39)

Clearly, these theories hinge on the concept of adult maturity and accompanying changes in experience. Davenport and Davenport paraphrase Carlson, dictating the appropriateness of adult education for "persons reaching adulthood, which is the point when society confers the legal and social rights and responsibilities of adulthood . . ." (1985, p. 155). Society confers adulthood on minors at eighteen, holding them responsible in an adult court of law, financially independent from their parents (varying on individual circumstance), and granting them the vote. Many, and increasingly more, battered women are in such circumstances. The premise of this section is based on what might initially seem a trivial consideration—the differences between andragogy and pedagogy. Adult educators believe, fundamentally, that adults learn differently from children. Far from a mere word game, this difference speaks volumes about the way we view education. In general use, pedagogy is used synonymously with 'teaching.' In its

129

more specific use, andragogy is the education of adults, while pedagogy is the education of children.

This basic tenet of adult education, or andragogy, has broad implications. I will consider the impact of this belief on four areas: the purpose of education, the framing of the learner, the role of the educator, and the process through which learning occurs. This chapter will review these four themes in adult education, contrast these with typical education, and illustrate the ways in which domestic violence shelters closely approximate these principles. Its purpose is not to presuppose that the theory of adult education be adopted wholesale, but to propose that principles of andragogy can assist in reconceptualizing and expanding informal education.

A Question of Purpose

The purpose and meaning of education is not a new question. In dialogues at least as early as 390 B.C., the time of Plato's *Meno*, scholars debated what the nature of learning was. The work of several theorists on this defining question has been particularly embraced by the adult education field. Perhaps best known outside the field is the writing of Paolo Freire, especially his oft-cited *Pedagogy of the Oppressed*. The purpose of Freire's educational practices in Brazil are clearly political; Freire taught peasants to read in order that their consciousnesses would be raised (conscientization).

> Conscientization is first of all the effort to enlighten men about the obstacles preventing them from a clear perception of reality. In this role, conscientization effects the ejection of cultural myths that confuse the people's awareness and make them ambiguous beings. (Freire 1970, p. 89)

Much work in political education follows this Freirian use of education for 'critical consciousness,' including the work of many feminists (cf. Jeanne Brady Giroux 1989; Sue Middleton 1993) and critical pedagogues such as Michael Apple (1993) and Henry Giroux (1988). However, adult education is not necessarily about raising *political* consciousness. Jack Mezirow states that learning is a:

> Dialectical process of interpretation in which we interact with objects and events, guided by an old set of expectations. . . . In transformative learning, however, we reinterpret an old experience (or a new one) from a new set of expectations, thus giving a new meaning and perspective to the old experience. (1991, p. 11 cited in Glyna Olson and Paul Kleine 1993)

Transformative learning is the consciousness-raising, the conscientization, of adult education. It reframes experience in new ways. This can be political, but it encompasses a broader agenda. For example, Mezirow speaks of life changes in adults "that precipitate critical reflection and transformation" (1990, p. 14). Life changes, or trigger events, in a recent paper by Carolyn Clark (1993) included realization of alcohol addiction and the birth of a child as experiences that transformed these adult learners' conceptions of their lives. Transformation in adult education both includes politics and means more, or as Mezirow writes,

> Transformation theory includes reflection on sociolinguistic assumptions and praxis but also encompasses reflection on epistemic and psychological assumptions. (1991, p. 251)

If Freire's construction of the purpose of education is too narrow to describe the category of adult education, what is that purpose? Mezirow says that "in essence, the purpose of learning is to enable us to understand the meaning of our experiences and to realize values in our lives" (1985, p. 17). This definition is both overly psychological and vague, and has many critics. The theory has been critiqued for its lack of social responsibility (cf. Phyllis Cunningham 1992) and for its apparent lack of consideration of the power issues inherent in the Habermasian theories that adult education, and Mezirow, espouse (cf. Mechthild Hart 1985). Given these objections, it may be simpler to determine the purpose of adult education by reflecting on simple logistics—how and where it is practiced. Since adult education is concerned with the education of the general category of adults, it is practiced in many different physical settings. One recent article describes "perspective transformation themes among rural mid-life college students," speaking of 'returning students' at the university (Olson and Kleine 1993), while in a 1988 article Malcolm Knowles discusses adult education in the context of on-the-job training. These two examples serve to illustrate the range of applicability encompassed by a general theory of adult education. This broadness of perspective is important in how the field of adult education defines itself: adult education serves the needs and purposes of the adult. *Adult education is what the adult wants it to be—it is a choice, defined by the adult.*

The drama of this last statement intentionally highlights the possibility of transformational learning, grounded in experience, to inform and raise consciousness. Without challenging the politics of the existence of a standard curriculum, it is still possible to create spaces in which transformative learning can take place. Maxine Greene urges us to "think of learning and teaching as spaces where persons can experience themselves as 'taking risks as embarking on new beginnings that will make the predictable give way to the possible'" (1989, cited in Mary Poplin 1993). These possibilities can best be seen through a reframing of the educator and the student.

Profile of an Adult Learner and an Adult Educator

Taking an andragogical look at the traditional teacher requires dramatic revisioning. The role of the teacher in adult learning is neither omniscient nor omnipotent. In a world of expanding information and racing technology, this would seem to be clear for all those who teach; however, judging from the resistance to this idea seen in typical school teaching practices it is far from casually accepted. Mary Daly reminds us that even the language used to discuss teaching reveals the "methodolatry" to which we are so religiously committed; to reveal one's lack of universal knowledge is not 'the way it spozed to be' (Daly 1973). In adult education the teacher is both student and teacher and the student is both teacher and student (Freire 1970), making the learning relationship clearly reciprocal. This experience of co-learning is important because it values the experience of both teacher and student, rather than the teacher-as-expert with all the valuable knowledge that must be imparted in some means to the student-with-no-knowledge. Along these lines, Kathy Scott, a feminist professor of education (1993) writes of her own experience of becoming a teacher/learner/researcher, moving beyond a vision of herself as merely the teacher to a multiplicity of roles. This redefinition must take place for both student and teacher, since the education of adults takes a very different form than the education of children. In domestic violence shelters, this gradual slope is evident in the transition from "new" resident to more established women. It is in these more established women, furthermore, that learning begins to be handed backwards from resident to resident. The typical pattern is from resident who has "been there" to newer resident.

Redefining the Adult Learner

The adult learner is self-directed. In fact, Mezirow writes that "[a]n adult has been defined as one who fulfills adult social roles and who sees himself or herself as a self-directed person" (1985, p. 17). According to Malcolm Knowles, self-directed learning is a process very different from that practiced in undergraduate classrooms. It is "a process in which individuals take the initiative without the help of others in diagnosing their learning needs, formulating goals, identifying human and material resources, and evaluating learning outcomes" (1975, p. 18). These conditions are not practiced within, and according to Peter Elbow (1986) are incompatible with the college classroom, yet are common within community-based education.

The transition into a self-directed learning mode is difficult and requires assistance. However, the necessity of assistance implies that the task can be done with that assistance, and eventually alone. This is in part the role of the adult educator—to provide the assistance that is needed and to withdraw excessive support. Again, the scaffolding metaphor is relevant. A scaffold is erected around a building during construction. Its support is sturdy, but not excessive, and as the building becomes complete, the scaffolding is gradually diminished along with the progress of the construction.

Redefining the Adult Educator

In order to be able to both judge the amount of support needed and to withdraw unnecessary authority, the teacher must her/himself be self-reflective. In fact, the concept of reflective practitioning usefully describes the relationship between teacher and student, and the teaching-learning relationship, in andragogy.

Reflective practitioning as a theory places the practitioner (in this case, the counselor, volunteer, or social worker) in a learning position. She is learning from practice, from the students and the situation. This concept partially deconstructs the power hierarchy of the traditional teaching-learning relationship. When it becomes clear that learning is truly a lifelong process, as adult education emphasizes, then the teacher truly is student and the student truly is teacher. This realization should be communicated to the students, both to allow them to see the continuous process and to realize that they are participating in that process, contributing to the learning of another. Were education students to see this relationship in their university classroom from the professor, and were they to learn it for themselves through practice, perhaps they would carry the notion of co-learning with them into the schoolroom. Lifelong learning as a conceptual framework for constant revision of and addition to knowledge also legitimates not-knowing. If learning is a lifelong process, it is not important to know everything *right now*, nor is such an admission a liability. Instead learning becomes a dialectical relationship between teacher-student and student-teacher in which each learns from the other. Reflective practitioning engenders a more participative process, including both teacher and students in a relationship of learning. Andragogy demands that both the role of the teacher and the student be redefined so that each participates in a unique way in the learning process.

In andragogy, reflection is encountered through the work of Habermas. As Mezirow writes, drawing on Habermas:

Knowledge gained through self-reflective learning is appraisive rather than prescriptive or designative. Action is emancipatory. The learner is presented with an alternative way of interpreting feelings and patterns of action; the old meaning scheme or perspective is reorganized to incorporate new insights; we come to see our reality more inclusively, to understand it more clearly, and to integrate our experience better. (1985, p. 21)

This statement makes several previously discussed concepts clear. First, andragogy relies on self-understanding (appraisal) and critique rather than externally imposed judgment. Second, learning is transformative. And third, learning is based in experience. Hart has criticized Mezirow on the basis of her reading of Habermas, which is much more politically charged. She writes that Habermas is "a body of theory and writing which ultimately leads to a questioning of the entire normative base of our social and economic arrangements" (1990, p. 126). It is important to Hart that andragogy be recognized as critical reflexivity, and that

critical reflexivity has precisely the purpose to examine how under current social and political circumstances, 'difference' always implies inequality, and that a positive acknowledgment of difference has to be inserted in a critique of the way inequality has shaped and determined many of the concrete manifestations of such difference. (Hart 1990, p. 135)

This critique of Mezirow is explicitly feminist, connecting andragogy with both feminist theory and pedagogy and the accompanying critique of power. As a feminist I agree that all education is politically charged. In no space is this as clear as in shelters, where politics shapes women's realities at all levels. It is politics that allows domestic violence to exist; politics that denies women many resources to redress their domestic violence-based problems; and politics that continues to constrain their lives as they move out of violence and search for better lives.

From Theory to Practice

Andragogy emphasizes self-directed learning, the immediate application of knowledge, utilization of life experiences, and problem-centered learning. These principles are currently utilized in battered women's shelters as well as the more commonly encountered experiences of staff development programs, continuing education, literacy programs, and other "adult" learning enterprises. The practice of andragogy focuses around these concepts and is critically linked to participation by the learner in the learning process. The practice of andragogy, then, has common elements such as critical reflection, self-direction, and a base in experience, but divergent ideas on the purposes of each of these methods.

Student voice is also foundational to andragogy. One of Freire's tenets is that there has long existed a "culture of silence" in which the experiences of the disenfranchised worker (in Brazil) were discounted. One of the radical notions Freire put into practice was his idea that these workers not only had experience but that their education could and should be based upon it. This same culture of silence has been discussed in recent years concerning the education of women (cf. AAUW 1991), the moral and ethical decisions of women (Carol Gilligan 1982), and the experiences of African-American students in the academy (cf. Signithia Fordham 1993). This reclamation of narrative for one's own use has been characterized by Madeline Grumet (1988) as a pedagogy of resistance. Utilizing women's (students') own experiences as a basis for learning is an andragogical —and liberatory—concept.

These experiences are foundational to learning in domestic violence shelters. First, women's own experience becomes the central component of their subsequent learning experiences. If they are silent, they learn to speak freely. If they lack parenting skills, they can learn new skills in that area. Second, women are surrounded by "authentic" staff—that is, staff who understand domestic violence and some of whom have experienced it themselves. The degree to which women interact with these staff, and need the authenticity, is another individual variant. Third, women are encouraged through a variety of means (see chapter 6 for one example) to tell their experiences—both within the shelter to other residents and outside the shelter, to public audiences. In these acts, feminist empowerment education meets, and combines, with the concepts of andragogy.

Feminism and Andragogy

As a feminist educator, it is important to me to point out the relationship of many of the concepts discussed thus far as andragogy to feminist pedagogy and feminist research. Conscientization, or consciousness-raising is a concept inextricably linked with the women's movement of the 1960s and 1970s (on community-building through CR, see chapter 2). In fact, Sue Middleton writes a defense of CR in her 1993 text: "[P]eople may describe their lives—their circumstances, their choices, their activities, their ideas—in ways they have not done before. In this they may make connections between the personal (an event or emotion) and the political or social" (p. 75). This is the same concept taken up in critical andragogy, discussed by Mezirow and politically strengthened by Hart. This connection is acknowledged by Mezirow (1989). "Consciousness raising in the women's movement and elsewhere is another example of adult education for perspective transformation" (p. 196).

However, the connections between feminist theory and andragogy reach further than CR. Reading critical andragogy resonates soundly with both critical and feminist pedagogy. (These writers mean pedagogy in the broad sense rather than the specific sense, separating adults from children, in which this chapter has used the term.) Feminist pedagogy assumes the worthwhile nature of women's, and students', experiences and attempts to decenter the traditional authority in the classroom (cf. Kathy Scott 1991). Feminist pedagogy further assumes that the student is capable of, and desires to, learn and understand both herself and the social structure in which she is embedded, thus carrying out Habermas's political purpose. The culture of silence of which Freire writes vividly describes peasant workers in Brazil. However, feminist writers found, and continue to find, a culture of silence in our schools (AAUW 1991; Lois Weis and Michelle Fine 1993); in our research (Michelle Fine 1992); and in women's lives (Carol Gilligan 1982).

Whether this connection is obscured because of the physical separation of andragogy from feminist theory or because of politics, it is clear that each body of theory calls on similar ideas about learning and the learner. Andragogy and feminism each define the purpose of education as liberation, whether from patriarchy or from rigidly hierarchical learning structures. Education is to free the person, enabling her to understand and counter her oppression or to accomplish her new goals. Rather than setting up oppositional theories or speculating on which was first to develop liberation as a concept, it is useful to recognize the connections between goals, purposes, and method among these different theories. This allows both bodies of knowledge to serve as resource for the restructuring of education and a strengthening of purpose.

Question Assumptions

Andragogy demands that we question our assumptions about the role of a teacher in a learning situation, and rethink the way learning takes place. Andragogical methods foster participation, such as a focus on women's experiences as curriculum. This and other processes inherently involve the student in a more participative process. Andragogy and feminism, although largely unrecognized as connected theories, owe much to each other. The links between feminist theory and andragogy emphasize cross-fertilization of ideas for different purposes. While feminism and feminist pedagogy lead toward the liberation of women, critical andragogy leads toward the participative education of adults. The similarity of these concepts, especially as used by Freire, allows a redefinition and extension of both theories; feminism encompasses both women and men, and andragogy may be also used in the "typical" college classroom. As feminist theorists and curriculum revisionists rethink many kinds and levels of education, the concepts of andragogy should be employed, with a focus on reflective practice, in order to raise our collective consciousness about the way women should teach and be taught. As feminist theorists rethink education, the domestic violence movement serves as one example in which concepts of andragogy are employed, together with reflective practice, to raise the collective consciousness about ways of both teaching and learning. In order to change the direction of progress, shelters change the direction of education, beginning where the women are, grounded in their own experience.

References

Abu-Lughod, L. (1995). A community of secrets: The separate world of Bedouin women. In P. A. Weiss, and M. Friedman. (1995) *Feminism & Community*. Philadelphia: Temple University Press.

Acker, J. (1990). Hierarchies, jobs, bodies: A theory of gendered organizations. *Gender & Society*, 4(1): 139–158.

American Association of University Women (1992). *How Schools Shortchange Girls*. Washington, DC: AAUW.

American Association of University Women. Researched by C. Sattler; R. Kirshstein; E. Rowe; E. DeFur; and K. Kleimann. (1998). *Gender Gaps: Where Schools Still Fail Our Children*. Washington, DC: AAUW.

Apple, M. (1993). *Official Knowledge: Democratic Education in a Conservative Age*. New York: Routledge.

Ashcroft, L. (1987). Defusing "empowering": The what and the why. *Language Arts, 64*: 142–156.

Asian Women United of California (Eds.) (1989). *Making Waves. An Anthology of Writings By and About Asian American Women*. Boston: Beacon.

Atkin, A.M. (1996). When Pincushions are Periodicals: Women's Work, Race, and Material Objects in Female Abolitionism. Unpublished manuscript.

Avery, B. Y. (1995). Breathing life into ourselves: The evolution of the national Black women's health project. In P. A. Weiss and M. Friedman, (1995) *Feminism & Community*. Philadelphia: Temple University Press.

Baker, D., and J. Snodgrass (1979). Team teaching a sociology of sex roles seminar: Using consciousness-raising methods. *Teaching Sociology* 6: 259–266.

Barkan, S. E. (1979). Strategic, tactical and organizational dilemmas of the protest movement against nuclear power. *Social Problems* 27: 19–37.

Bart, P.B. (1995). Seizing the means of reproduction: An illegal feminist abortion collective—how and why it worked. in P. A. Weiss, and M. Friedman, *Feminism & Community*. Philadelphia: Temple University Press.

Bart, P. B. and E. G. Moran (Eds.) (1993). *Violence Against Women. The Bloody Footprints*. Newbury Park, CA: Sage.

Bateson, M. C. (1990). *Composing a Life*. New York: Penguin.

Beaudry, M. (1985). *Battered Women*. Translated by L. Huston and M. Heap, Montreal: Black Rose Books.

Behar, R. (1997). *The Vulnerable Observer: Anthropology That Breaks Your Heart*. Boston: Beacon.

Belenkey, M. F., B. M. Clinchy, N. R. Goldberger, and J. M. Tarule. (1987). *Women's Ways of Knowing*. BasicBooks.

Berry, D. B. (1996). *Domestic Violence Sourcebook*. Los Angeles: Lowell House.

Bitensky, Robert. (1975). From apathy to social activism. *Inquiry* 18: 213–223.

Blumberg, R. L. (1991). *Gender, Family, and Economy: The Triple Overlap*. Newbury Park, CA: Sage.

Boston Women's Health Collective (1992). *The New Our Bodies, Ourselves*. New York: Touchstone.

Boxer, M. J. (1982). For and about women: The theory and practice of women's studies in the united states. *Signs: Journal of Women and Culture in Society, 7(3)*: 661–695.

Broude, N., and M. D. Garrard, (1994). *The Power of Feminist Art. The American Movement of the 1970s, History and Impact*. New York: Harry N. Abrams.

Brown, C. (1992). Healing pain and building bridges. *Women of Power* 22: 16–21.

Brown, L, F. Dubau, and M. McKeon. (1997). *Stop Domestic Violence: An Action Plan for Saving Lives*. New York: St. Martin's Griffin.

Brown, R.M. (1995). The furies collective. in P. A. Weiss and M. Friedman. (1995) *Feminism & Community*. Philadelphia: Temple University Press.

Bunch, C. (1987). *Passionate Politics. Feminist Theory in Action*. New York: St. Martins Press.

Bunch, C. and S. Pollack. (Eds). (1983). *Learning our Way: Essays in Feminist Education*. Trumansburg, NY: Crossingburg Press.

Buzawa, E.S., and C. G. Buzawa. (1996). *Domestic Violence. The Criminal Justice Response*. Thousand Oaks, CA: Sage.

Cape Cod Chronicle (March 31, 1994). "Silent no more: A witness against violence erected at Harwich High School."

Cape Cod Times (October 30, 1994). "A lesson in painful reality. Clothesline Project's domestic violence display chills students."

Casey, K. (1993). *I Answer With my Life. Life Histories of Women Teachers Working for Social Change*. New York: Routledge.

Chafetz, J. S. (1984). *Sex and Advantage: A Comparative, Macro-structural Theory of Sex Stratification*. Totowa, NJ: Rowman and Allanheld.

Chafetz, J. S. (1991). The gender division of labor and the reproduction of female disadvantage. In R. Blumberg (ed.), *Gender, Family, and Economy: The Triple Overlap*. Newbury Park, CA: Sage.

Chafetz, J. S. and Dworkin, A. G. (1986). *Female Revolt: Women's Movements in World and Historical Perspective*. Totowa, NJ: Rowman & Allanheld.

Chapman, T. (1988). "Behind the Wall" *Tracy Chapman*, Tracy Chapman. Wea/Elektra Entertainment.

Chicago, J. 1980. *Embroidering Our Heritage. The Dinner Party Needlework*. New York: Anchor Press.

Chicago, J. (1996). *The Dinner Party (a commemorative volume celebrating a major monument of twentieth-century art)*. New York: Penguin.

Clark, M. C. (1993). *Changing course: Initiating the transformational learning process*. Paper presented at the Thirty-Fourth Annual Adult Education Research Conference, Pennsylvania State University.

Clothesline Project (1995). Press kit.

Collier, J. F. and S. J. Yanagisako. (1988). Theory in anthropology since feminist practice. *Critique of Anthropology* 9(2): 27–37.

Crane, V., H. Nicholson, M. Chen, S. Bitgood. (1994). *Informal Science Learning: What the research says about television, science museums, and community-based projects*. Denham, MA: Research Communications, Ltd. Science Press.

Crawford, M. and M. MacLeod. (1990). Gender in the college classroom: An assessment of the "chilly climate" for women. *Sex Roles, 23(3/4)*: 101–122.

Crowell, N. A., and A.W. Burgess. (Eds.) (1996). *Understanding Violence Against Women*. Panel on Research on Violence Against Women; Committee on Law and Justice; Commission on Behavioral and Social Sciences and Education. Washington, DC: National Academy Press.

Cunningham, P. M. (1992). *From Freire to feminism: The North American experience with critical pedagogy. Adult Education Quarterly*, 42(2): 180–191.

Currie, D., and H. Kazi. (1987). "Academic feminism and the process of deradicalization: Re-examining the issues." *Feminist Review*: 77–98.

Daly, M. (1973). *Beyond God the Father. Toward a Philosophy of Women's Liberation*. Boston: Beacon Press.

Datnow, A. (1998). *The Gender Politics of Educational Change*. Educational Change and Development Series. London: Falmer.

Davenport, J., and J. A. Davenport. (1985). *A chronology and analysis of the andragogy debate. Adult Education Quarterly*, 35(3): 152–159.

Dennis Register (February 16, 1995). "Few words spoken as Wixon students view clothesline project."

Dominy, M. D. (1986). "Lesbian-feminist gender conceptions: separatism in Christchurch, New Zealand." *Signs: Journal of Women in Culture and Society*, 11: 274–289.

DuBois, E. C., G.P. Kelly, E.L. Kennedy, C.W. Korsmeyer, and L.S. Robinson. (1985). *Feminist Scholarship: Kindling in the Groves of Academia*. Chicago: University of Illinois Press.

Duke, D., and D. Harding. (Eds.) (1987). *America's Glorious Quilts*. China: Hugh Lauter Levin Associates Inc.

DuPlessis, R.B. (1979). The feminist apologues of Lessing, Piercy, and Russ. *Frontiers*, 6(1): 1–8.

Durkheim, Emile. (1915). *The Elementary Forms of the Religious Experience*. New York: Free Press.

———. (1951). *Suicide*. New York: Free Press.

Dutton, D. G. (1995). *The Domestic Assault of Women. Psychological and Criminal Justice Perspectives*. Vancouver: University of British Columbia Press.

Dworkin, A. and C. Mackinnon. (1985). Text of the Dworkin-Mackinnon Ordinance, pp. 334-345 in K. Kahn. (Ed.). *Front Line Feminism, 1975–1995, Essays from Sojourner's First 20 Years*. San Francisco: Aunt Lute Books.

Easteal, P. (1994). *Voices of the Survivors*. North Melbourne, Australia: Spinifex Press.

Easton, P.A. (1989). Structuring learning environments: Lessons from the organization of post-literacy programs. *International Review of Education, 35*: 423–444.

Eisler, R. (1987). *The Chalice & the Blade. Our History, Our Future*. Cambridge, Mass.: Harper & Row.

Elbow, P. (1986). The pedagogy of the bamboozled. In P. Elbow (ed.). *Embracing Contraries*. London: Oxford University Press.

Elslasser, N, K. and Mackenzie, and Y. Tixier y Vigil, (1980). *Las Mujeres. Conversations from a Hispanic Community*. New York: The Feminist Press at the City University of New York.

Epstein, C. F. (1975). *Ten years later: perspectives on the women's movement. Dissent* (Spring), 169–176.

Evans, S. (1979). *Personal Politics: The Roots of Women's Liberation in the Civil Rights Movement and the New Left.* New York: Knopf.

Falk, J.H., and L.D. Dierking. (1993a). *Public Institutions for Personal Learning: Understanding the Long-term Impact of Museums.* Washington, DC: Howells House.

Falk, J.H., and L.D. Dierking. (1993b). *The Museum Experience.* Washington, DC: Howells House.

Faludi, S. (1991). *Backlash: The Undeclared War Against American Women.* New York: Crown.

Fine, M. (1992). *Disruptive Voices: The Possibilities of Feminist Research.* Ann Arbor: University of Michigan Press.

Firestone, S. (1972). *The Dialectic of Sex: The Case for Feminist Revolution.* New York: Bantam/William Morrow & Co.

Ford Foundation. (1992). *Violence Against Women: Addressing a Global Problem.* New York, NY: Ford Foundation.

Fordham, S. (1993). Those loud black girls: (Black) women, silence, and gender passing in the academy. *Anthropology and Education Quarterly*, 24(1): 3–32.

Foucault, M. (1962). *Madness and Civilization.* New York: Pantheon.

———. (1975). *Discipline and Punish.* London: Tavistock.

———. (1977). *Language, Counter-Memory, Practice.* Ithaca, NY: Cornell University Press.

———. (1978). *The History of Sexuality.* New York: Vintage Books.

Freedman, E. (1995). Separatism as strategy: Female institution building and American feminism, 1970–1930. in P. A. Weiss, and M. Friedman, *Feminism & Community.* Philadelphia: Temple University Press.

Freeman, J. (1975). *The Politics of Women's Liberation: A Case Study of an Emerging Social Movement and Its Relation to the Policy Process.* New York: Longman.

———. (1979). Resource movilization and strategy: A model for analyzing social movement organizations. In M.N. Zald, and J. D. McCarthy, (eds.). *The Dynamics of Social Movements*, pp. 57–189. Cambridge, MA: Winthrop.

———. (1984). *Women. A Feminist Perspective.* California: Mayfield Pt. CO.

Freire, Paolo. (1970). *Pedagogy of the Oppressed.* New York: Continuum.

Gaynor, G. (1979). *I Will Survive.* Sound recording.

Gennaro, E.E. (1982). *Out-of-School Science Learning Experiences for Parents and their Middle School Children: Introduction (a course for parents and children)*, Washington, DC: National Science Foundation.

Gilligan, C. (1982). *In a Different Voice*. Cambridge: Harvard University Press.

Gilligan, C. J. V. Ward, and J. M. Taylor. (1988). *Mapping the Moral Domain*. Cambridge: Harvard University Press.

Giroux, H.A. (1988). *Schooling and the Struggle for Public Life*. Minneapolis: University of Minnesota Press.

Giroux, J. B. (1989). Feminist theory as pedagogical practice. *Contemporary Education, 61*: 6–10.

Glaspell, S. (1993) *A Jury of Her Peers*. Wan Kato, Minn.: Creative Education, Inc.

Gore, J. (1993). *The Struggle for Pedagogies. Critical and Feminist Discourses as Regimes of Truth*. New York: Routledge.

Griffin, G. (1992). *Calling: Essays on Teaching in the Mother Tongue*. Pasadena, California: Trilogy Books.

Grumet, Madeline. (1988). *Bitter Milk: Women and Teaching*. Amherst: University of Massachusetts Press.

Gumport, P. J. (1990). Feminist scholarship as a vocation. *Higher Education*, 20(2): 231–243.

Hart, M. (1985). Thematization of power, the search for common interests, and self-reflection: Towards a comprehensive concept of emancipatory education. *International Journal of Lifelong Education*, 4: 119–134.

————. (1990). Critical theory and beyond: Further perspectives on emancipatory education. *Adult Education Quarterly*, 40(3): 125–138.

Hartmann, H. I. (1981). "The Unhappy Marriage of Marxism and Feminism: Towards a More Progressive Union." In Alison M. Jaggar, and Paula Rothenberg (eds.). *Feminist Frameworks*. New York: McGraw-Hill, 172–189.

Harwich Oracle (April 1, 1994). "Harwich High is first school to display Clothesline Project."

Helly, D. O., and S.M. Reverby. (Eds.). (1992). *Gendered Domains. Rethinking Public and Private in Women's History*. Ithaca, NY: Cornell University Press.

Honig, E. (1995). Burning incense, pledging sisterhood: Communities of women workers in the Shanghai cotton mills, 1919–1949. In P. A. Weiss, and M. Friedman. (1995) *Feminism & Community*. Philadelphia: Temple University Press.

hooks, b. (1984). *Feminist Theory: From Margin to Center*. Boston: South End Press.

————. (1994). *Teaching to Transgress. Education as the Practice of Freedom*. New York: Routledge.

Hyde, C. (1986). Experiences of women activists: Implications for community organizing theory and practice. *Journal of Sociology and Social Welfare* 13: 545–562.

Jacobson, S. K. (1990). A model for using a developing country's park system for conservation education. *Journal of Environmental Education* 22(1): 19–25.

Jaggar, A. M. (1988). *Feminist Politics and Human Nature*. Totowa, NJ: Rowman & Allanheld.

Jones, A. (1994). *Next Time, She'll be Dead: Battering and How To Stop It*. Boston: Beacon.

Kahn, K. (1995). *Front Line Feminism, 1975–1995. Essays From Sojourner's First 20 Years*. San Francisco: Aunt Lute Books.

Kamen, P. (1991). *Feminist Fatale*. New York: Donald I. Fine.

Kaplan, L. (1995). *The Story of Jane, the Legendary Underground Feminist Abortion Service*. Chicago: University of Chicago Press.

Kehoe, A. B. (1990). Gender is an organon. *Zygon* 25: 139–150.

Kemter, A. (1989). Hidden power in marriage. *Gender & Society*, 3(2): 187–216.

Kerber, L. (1988). Separate spheres, female worlds, woman's place: The rhetoric of women's history. *Journal of American History* 75(June): 9–39.

Klein, E. (1984). *Gender Politics: From Consciousness to Mass Politics*. Cambridge: Harvard University Press.

Knowles, M. (1975). *Self-directed Learning: A Guide for Learners and Teachers*. New York: Cambridge University Press.

Knowles, M. S. (1970). *The Modern Practice of Adult Education: Andragogy versus Pedagogy*. New York: Association Press.

———. (1988, August). Everything you wanted to know from Malcolm Knowles (and weren't afraid to ask). *Training*, 45–50.

Konek, C. W. (1996). "*Listen.*" Unpublished poem.

Kresiberg, S. (1992). *Transforming Power: Domination, Empowerment, and Education*. Albany: SUNY Press.

Lehmann, J. M. (1990). Durkheim's response to feminism: Prescriptions for women. *Sociological Theory* 8: 163–187.

Lems, Kristen. (1980). *Never Give Up*. sound recording.

Lewis, M. G. (1993). *Without a Word. Teaching Beyond Women's Silence*. New York: Routledge.

Lockwood, J. H. (1996). The moral of the story: Content, process, and reflection in moral education through narrative. Unpublished dissertation manuscript, University of Florida, Gainesville, Florida.

Lorde, A. (1981). The master's tools will never dismantle the master's house. In *This Bridge Called My Back*. Cherrie Moraga and Gloria

Anzaldua (Eds.), 98–106. New York: Kitchen Table: Women of Color Press.

Luke, C. (1996) (Ed.). *Feminisms and Pedagogies of Everyday Life*. Albany: SUNY Press.

Luker, K. (1984). Motherhood and morality in America. in *Abortion and the Politics of Motherhood*. Berkeley: University of California Press, pp. 192–215.

Manning, P. K. (1991). Semiotic ethnographic research. *American Journal of Semiotics* 8: 27–45.

Marcus, J. (1982). Storming the toolshed. *Signs: Journal of Women in Culture and Society, 7(3)*: 622–640.

Mariani, C. (1996). *Domestic Violence Survival Guide*. New York: Looseleaf Law Publications.

Martin, D. (1976). *Battered Wives*. Volcano, CA: Volcano Press.

———. (1995). A letter from a battered wife. in P. A. Weiss, and M. Friedman. *Feminism & Community*. Philadelphia: Temple University Press.

Martin, J. R. (1994). *Changing the Educational Landscape*. New York: Routledge.

Martin, P. Y. (1991). Feminism and management. In *Women in Management: Trends, Perspectives, and Challenges*. E. Fagenson (ed.). Newbury Park, CA: Sage.

Maryland Men's Anti-Rape Resource Center (1995). Press kit.

McEwan, E. K. (1992). *My Mother, My Daughter: Women Speak Out*. Wheaton, IL.: Harold Shaw Publishers.

Mezirow, J. (1985). *A critical theory of self-directed learning. New Directions for Continuing Education* 25(3): 17–30.

———. (1990). *Fostering Critical Reflection in Adulthood*. San Francisco: Jossey-Bass.

———. (1992). Transformation theory: Critique and confusion. *Adult Education Quarterly*, 42(4): 250–252.

Middleton, S. (1993). *Educating Feminists*. New York: Teacher's College Press.

Miller, J. L. (1990). *Creating Spaces and Finding Voices. Teachers Collaborating for Empowerment*. Albany: SUNY Press.

Morgan, R. (Ed.). (1992). Twentieth anniversary issue. *Ms. Magazine, 3(1)*.

Morgan, Robin. (1970). *Sisterhood Is Powerful*. New York: Vintage.

Morris, A. D., and C. M. Mueller. (1992). *Frontiers in Social Movement Theory*. New Haven: Yale University Press.

Mullin, M. (1991). Representations of history, Irish feminism, and the politics of difference. *Feminist Studies* 17: 29–50.

National Organization for Women. (1992). Newsletter.

Newman, R. (1998). *Go Down, Moses. Celebrating the African-American Spiritual.* New York: Roundtable Press.

NOW Times (June 1995). Newspaper.

Ogbu, J. (1978). *Minority Education and Caste: The American System in Cross-cultural Perspective.* New York: Academic Press.

Olsen, T. (1978). *Silences.* New York: Dell.

Olson, G., and P. Kleine. (1993). *Perspective transformation themes among rural midlife college students: Subtle vs. dramatic changes.* Paper presented at the Thirty-Fourth Annual Adult Education Research Conference, Pennsylvania State University.

Orenstein, P. (1994). *Schoolgirls. Young Women, Self–Esteem, and the Confidence Gap.* New York: Doubleday.

Osmond, M. W., and B. Thorne. (1993). Feminist theories: The social construction of gender in families and society. In Pauline G. Boss, William J. Doherty, Ralph LaRossa, Walter R. Schumm, and Suzanne K. Steimetz. (eds.) *Sourcebook of Family Theories and Methods.* New York: Plenum Press.

Otto, W. (1994). *How to Make an American Quilt.* New York, NY: Ballentine Books.

Peshkin, A. (1988). In search of subjectivity—one's own. *Educational Researcher*, 17(9): 17–22.

Pierce, S., and V. Suite. (1994). *Art Quilts: Playing with a Full Deck.* San Francisco: Pomegranite Art Books.

Pipher, M. (1994). *Reviving Ophelia. Saving the Selves of Adolescent Girls.* New York: Ballantine.

Refuge House. (1992). Training manual.

Rich, A. (1979) *On Lies, Secrets, and Silence.* New York: W.W. Norton.

Ringgold, F. (1995). *We Flew Over the Bridge. The Memoirs of Faith Ringgold.* Boston: Little, Brown and Company.

Ringgold, F. (1998). *Dancing at the Louvre and other quilts from the French-American Collection.* Exhibition catalogue. Boston: Boston Museum of Art.

Rosaldo, M. (1974). A theoretical overview. in M. Rosaldo, and L. Lamphere. (Eds). *Woman, Culture, and Society,* pp. 23–24.

Rose, M. (1989). *Lives on the Boundary.* New York: Free Press.

Rosenberg, R. (1982). *Beyond Separate Spheres. The Intellectual Roots of Modern Feminism.* New Haven: Yale University Press.

Ruth, S. (1973). A serious look at consciousness-raising. *Social Theory and Practice* 2: 289–300.

Ryan, B. (1992) *Feminism and the Women's Movement: Dynamics of Change in Social Movement Ideology and Activism.* New York: Routledge.

Sadker, M., and D. Sadker. (1994) *Failing at Fairness. How Our Schools Cheat Girls.* New York: Simon & Schuster.

Sapon Shevin, M. (1993). Gifted education and the protection of privilege: Breaking the silence, opening the discourse. In L. Weis, and M. Fine. (Eds). *Beyond Silenced Voices. Class, Race, and Gender in United States Schools.* Albany: SUNY Press.

Sattler, C. L. (1996). Hearts-on learning: Thoughtful connections between formal and informal learning. Paper presented at the American Educational Research Association, New York, NY.

———. (1997). *Talking About a Revolution: The Politics and Practice of Feminist Teaching.* Cresskill, NJ: Hampton Press.

Schechter, S. (1982). *Women and Male Violence. The Visions and Struggles of the Battered Women's Movement.* Boston: South End Press.

Schwartz-Shea, P., and D. D. Burrington. (1990). Free riding, alternative organization and cultural feminism: The case of Seneca women's peace camp. *Women & Politics* 10: 1–37.

Scott, K. P. (1993). *Researching pedagogy: A transformative, feminist perspective.* Paper presented at the American Educational Research Association, Atlanta, Georgia.

Sharistanian, J. (Ed.) (1986). *Beyond the Public/domestic Dichotomy: Contemporary Perspectives on Women's Public Lives.* New York: Greenwood Press.

———. (Ed.) (1987). *Gender, Ideology, and Action: Historical Perspectives on Women's Public Lives.* New York: Greenwood Press.

Simon, R. (1988). For a pedagogy of possibility. *Critical Pedagogy Networker,* 1(1).

Sklar, K. K. (1973). *Catharine Beecher: A Study in American Domesticity.* New York: Norton.

———. (1995). *Florence Kelley and the Nation's Work: The Rise of Women's Political Culture, 1830–1900.* New Haven: Yale University Press.

Smith, B. (Ed.) (1983). *Home Girls. A Black Feminist Anthology.* New York: Kitchen Table: Women of Color Press.

Smith, William French. (1983). FBI statistics. In Refuge House, 1992, training manual.

Smithsonian Institution, Museum of American History (1996). Exhibit: From Parlor to Politics.

Snow, D., and R.D. Benford. (1988). Ideology, frame resonance, and participant mobilization. Pp. 197–217 in B. Klandermans, H. Y. Kriesi, S. Tarrow, (Eds.) *From Structure to Action: Social Movement*

Participation Across Cultures, International Social Movement Research, vol. 1. Greenwich, CT: JAI Press.

Snow, D., L. A. Zurcher, Jr. and A. Ekland-Olson. (1980). Social networks and social movements: A microstructural approach to differential recruitment. *American Sociological Review* 45: 787–801.

Snow, D., Rochford, Worden, and R.D.Benfor (1986). Frame alignment and mobilization. *American Sociological Review* 51(4): 464–481.

Spelman, E. (1988). *Inessential Woman*. Boston: Beacon Press.

Spender, D. (1980) *Man Made Language*. London: Pandora Press.

Stacey, J. (1988). "Can there be a feminist ethnography?" *Women's Studies International Forum*, 11(1): 21–27.

Staggensborg, S. (1987). Life-style preferences and social movement recruitment: illustrations from the abortion conflict. *Social Science Quarterly*, 68(4): 779–797.

———. (1989). Stability and innovation in the women's movement: a comparison of two movement organizations. *Social Problems*, 36(1): 75–92.

Statman, J. B. (1995). *The Battered Woman's Survival Guide—Breaking the Cycle*. Dallas: Taylor.

Steinem, G. 1983. *Outrageous Acts and Everyday Rebellions*. New York: Holt, Rinehart & Winston.

Tannen, D. (1988). *That's Not What I Meant/How Conversational Style Makes or Breaks Relationships*. New York: Ballantine Books.

———. (1991). *You Just Don't Understand/Women and Men in Conversation*. New York: Ballantine.

The Women's Political Action Group. (1992). *The Women's 1992 Voting Guide*. Berkeley: EarthWorks Press.

Tobin, J., and R. Dobard, (1999). *Hidden in Plain View. A Secret Story of Quilts and the Underground Railroad*. New York: Doubleday.

Tong, R. (1989). *Feminist Thought: A Comprehensive Introduction*. San Francisco: Westview Press.

Turner, T. (1984). *What's Love Got To Do With It?* Capitol Records, Inc. Sound recording.

Twerski, A. J. (1996). *The Shame Borne in Silence: Spouse Abuse in the Jewish Community*. Pittsburgh, PA: Mirkov Publications, Inc.

U.S. Department of Education. (1993). *Goals 2000 Workbook*. Washington, DC: Department of Education.

Vygotsky, L. S. (1978). *Mind in Society*. Cambridge: Harvard University Press.

Walker, L. (1979). *The Battered Woman*. New York: HarperPerennial.

Wallace, R. A. and Hartley, S. F. (1988). "Religious elements in Friendship: Durkehimian Theory in Empirical Context." In Jeffrey Alexander,

J., (Ed). *Durkheimian Sociology: Cultural Studies.* Cambridge: University of Cambridge Press, pp. 93–106.

Weeden in Giroux, Henry A. (1988). *Schooling and the Struggle for Public Life.* Minneapolis: University of Minnesota Press.

Weick, K.E. (1976). Educational organizations as loosely coupled systems. *Administrative Science Quarterly* 21, 1–19.

———. (1992). Administering education in loosely coupled schools. *Phi Delta Kappan*, 673–676.

Weis, L. (1993). White male working-class youth: An exploration of relative privilege and loss. In L. Weis, and M. Fine, (Eds). *Beyond Silenced Voices. Class, Race, and Gender in United States Schools.* Albany: SUNY Press.

Weis, L. & Fine, M. (Eds). (1993). *Beyond Silenced Voices. Class, Race, and Gender in United States Schools.* Albany: SUNY Press.

Weiss, P. A., and M. Friedman, (1995). *Feminism & Community.* Philadelphia: Temple University Press.

Welter, B. (1966). The cult of true womanhood, 1820–1860, *American Quarterly* 18 (Summer): 150–174.

Wolf, N. (1993). *Fire with Fire: The New Female Power and How it Will Change the 21st Century.* New York: Random House.

Woolf, V. (1952). *Three Guineas.* London: Hogarth Press.

———. (1957). *A Room of One's Own.* New York: Harcourt Brace Jovanovich.

Yin, R.K., K. Zantal-Wiener, and C.L. Sattler. (1998). *A report on the evaluation of the National Science Foundation's informal science education program.* Arlington, VA: National Science Foundation, NSF 98-65.

Zantal-Wiener, K., R.K. Yin, and C. Sattler. (1997). *The National Science Foundation's Informal Science Education Program Evaluation Report.* Washington, DC: COSMOS Corporation.

Index

abortion, 14, 20
adult learning, 129–137
American Association of University
  Women, 55
authority, 83

child care, 87
children, 114
Clothesline Project, xvii, 52, 67–77, 79
consciousness-raising, 18, 27–29,
  34–38, 40, 42–45, 85, 135–136
craft work, xvii, 16–18, 67, 98–99
credibility, 61–62
curriculum bias, 72
cycle of violence, 119

Dobard, Raymond, 9, 98–99
domestic sphere, 15, 17, 19, 67,
  103–104
domestic violence, xviii, xix, 2, 4–8, 25,
  93–94, 103–124
Douglass, Frederick, 99

economics, 110–111
emotional abuse, 112–113
employment, 89
empowerment, 33, 78–80

Faith Ringgold, 17, 65–66
feminist community, 10, 20, 77, 83–84
feminist teaching, xv, xix, 48–50,
  53–57, 77–78, 81, 135–136
Freire, Paolo, 64, 130–132, 137

Gere Lewis, Magda, 5, 32, 34, 37, 53,
  57
Goldman, Emma, 59

hooks, bell, 34, 44, 47–48, 85
housing, 87–88

informal education, 47, 49–52, 66,
  75–76, 85
intimidation, 112
isolation, 109–110

Knowles, Malcolm, 129, 131

language , 84–85
Lockwood, John, 32
Lorde, Audre, 28, 40, 57

MacKinnon, Catherine, 38
male privilege, 115
Mezirow, Jack, 130–132, 134
Miles, Angela, 32
minimizing, 113–114
Morgan, Robin, 35–36
mothering, 81
Mujeres Unidas en Accion, 57–59

National Organization of Women, 36
nonviolence, 117

physical abuse continuum, 115
power and control, 80, 116–117,
  122–128
public schools, xix, 75

quilting, xvi, xvii, 16–17, 35, 50, 65, 72, 98–100

restraining order, 32, 81
Rosser, Sue, 57

safe space, 14, 44
shelter, 23–24
shelter movement, 3, 4, 16, 20, 125–128
shelter workers, 41–42, 58–60, 62–63, 90–92
silence, 9–10, 27–28, 32, 69
slavery, vii, 1–4, 7–8, 10, 13, 24, 98–99, 125–128
stereotypes, 122–124

storytelling, 32–34, 36, 38–39, 43, 60–61, 66, 70
survival, 94–97

Tobin, Jacqueline, 9, 98–99
training, 59, 103–124
trust, 90–92
Turner, Tina, 109

underground railroad, xv, xvi, 2–4, 9–10, 13, 20, 79, 98, 100

voice, 27, 65, 83–85, 135

women's friendships, 18, 21, 22
women's groups, xvi, xvii, 2, 18–20, 22, 35–36, 50, 57–58, 70, 79